THE EMIGRANTS' GUIDE TO CALIFORNIA

LONDON: HUMPHREY MILFORD
OXFORD UNIVERSITY PRESS

Narratives of the Trans-Mississippi Frontier

THE EMIGRANTS' GUIDE TO CALIFORNIA

BY
JOSEPH E. WARE

Reprinted from the 1849 edition
With Introduction and Notes
by John Caughey

PRINCETON · PRINCETON UNIVERSITY PRESS · 1932

NARRATIVES OF THE TRANS-MISSISSIPPI FRONTIER

CARL L. CANNON, *General Editor*

ROUTE ACROSS THE ROCKY MOUNTAINS

By OVERTON JOHNSON *and* WM. H. WINTER

EDITED BY CARL L. CANNON

A JOURNAL OF THE SANTA FE EXPEDITION UNDER COLONEL DONIPHAN

By JACOB S. ROBINSON

EDITED BY CARL L. CANNON

THE EMIGRANTS' GUIDE TO CALIFORNIA

By JOSEPH E. WARE

EDITED BY JOHN CAUGHEY

THE PAST AND PRESENT OF THE PIKE'S PEAK GOLD REGIONS

By HENRY VILLARD

EDITED BY LE ROY R. HAFEN

Other volumes in preparation

PRINTED AT THE PRINCETON UNIVERSITY PRESS
PRINCETON, NEW JERSEY, U.S.A.

EDITOR'S PREFACE

WHEN the unsettling news that gold had been discovered in the strange land called California, reached the Mississippi and the Atlantic seaboard, the first question asked was, How can I get there? Until then, the widening stream of western emigration had been directed, for the most part, toward Oregon. California, two years before, had been a Mexican province, a land of sleepy peons, feudal cattle ranches, exotic fruits, unsuited, so it seemed, either for the Illinois plough, or the New England religion. Gold at once swept away all inhibitions and all obstacles, except those of distance and the cost of getting to Sacramento. Formidable problems these, when it is considered that most of the gold-seekers had little money and all wanted to reach Eldorado before the gold-bearing streams had been stripped by earlier arrivals.

Ware sensed the problem and its solution, at least for large numbers of fortune hunters California-bound, and published the first practical guide; a guide which gave the pros and cons of the different possible routes, as well as specific directions for reaching the goal by the quickest and cheapest one. For seafaring New Englanders, "around the Horn" was generally preferred, but the voyage consumed from six to nine months and cost $600—a large sum for those days. Southerners might go by way of Arizona, or, more likely, by Panama, with its tedious carry-over at the Strait, and attendant risks of congestion and cholera. This journey, moreover, from New York to San Francisco was six thousand miles in length, and, due to unfavorable conditions, proved expensive as well. From Independence, Missouri, to the gold fields, the trip, by the Plains, could be made in one hundred days, and, as Ware calculated it, for as low a cost as $55.19, provided the Argonaut traveled in partnership.

This land trip appealed to all farmers and artisans used to handling horses and oxen, especially if the traveling expense of a family had to be sustained. Although Americans had been drifting into California in small numbers for ten years or more, they had usually followed the Oregon trail beyond the passes of the Rockies and then made their way across the inland desert, and through the Sierras, by different routes—each striving for a cut-off.

From Fort Hall on the Oregon trail to California, the road was little known except to fur-trappers, and it was Ware's distinct contribution to guide literature that he first charted the trail with camping places over the unfamiliar stage of the journey. Professor Caughey, who has edited this volume, gives in his introduction a valuable analysis of early guides to the gold region.

Ware's guide appeared just when it was needed, and was used by hundreds who crossed the Plains in 'forty-nine. Since it is now one of the scarcest titles in the field of Western Americana, it must be assumed that most copies were worn out on the long, hard journey. Even, as in the following year, Ware himself, ill, weak and deserted by his companions, died on the trail near old Fort Laramie.

It is a pleasure to bring back into print the volume which is listed by Henry Wagner as one of the twenty rarest and most important volumes of Californiana.

Thanks are gladly given to the librarian of the Henry E. Huntington Library for permission to reproduce the text from the original in his possession.

C. L. C.

HISTORICAL INTRODUCTION

BY the close of *1848* California gold fever raged in every part of the United States. Suggested in January of that year when Marshall discovered gold, this fever had not become virulent even in California until May, when Sam Brannan's infectious shout, "Gold! Gold! Gold from the American River!" and his quinine bottle full of the precious dust started a rush from San Francisco. Although localized in California for a time, the gold fever was, nevertheless, intense; three-fourths of the men left the northern towns that spring. Before the end of the season the contagion had spread along and across the Pacific, to Hawaii, Oregon, Mexico, Peru, and Chile.

Gradually the excitement spread to the eastern United States and to Europe. Rumors and travelers' tales, California letters and newspapers aroused more than a passing interest in the States; Loesser's arrival as official messenger, with three thousand dollars' worth of gold dust in a tea-caddy, riveted this attention; and when President Polk in his message to Congress, on December 5, *1848*, took official cognizance of the great discovery, his words became the signal for a stampede to California.

California could be reached in a number of ways. Most New Englanders preferred the sea routes around Cape Horn or by Panama. From the southern States a good many traveled through Mexico. But for the midwesterners the overland trails were more proximate and

[ix]

convenient. The majority of the forty-niners, in fact, used the overland routes, the favorite being the Platte-South Pass-Humboldt-Truckee itinerary recommended in the guide-book herewith reprinted.

The major overland trails to California had been worked out before 1849. Santa Fe caravans, fur trappers, and Los Angeles pack trains had opened southern routes, which Kearny and Cooke made better known during the War with Mexico. A vanguard of fur men and Oregon missionaries had penetrated into the Rocky Mountains and the Great Basin, and had broken central and northern trails to Oregon and California. Following them during the forties, thousands of pioneer settlers took their covered wagons through South Pass on the road to Oregon, and hundreds turned off at Fort Hall to go down the Humboldt and across the Sierra to California. Meanwhile the Mormons broadened the trail up the Platte in their hegira from the States to Great Salt Lake, and Frémont trod old trails and experimented with new throughout the West. By 1849 most of the trail-blazing was already done; the forty-niners faced only the task of trail-following, except when, in their optimism, they attempted short-cuts and variations of the tested routes.

But though the trails were broken, most of the information thus accumulated was not conveniently available to the mid-westerners, who itched with the gold fever in the winter of 1848. The trappers, most avid of early western travelers, had been singularly reticent. Jed Smith, greatest of them all, apparently broke into print but once;[1] the average fur man not this often. Further-

[1] H. R. Wagner, *The Plains and the Rockies*, San Francisco, 1920, p. 24.

more, since the mountain men traveled ordinarily not with the intention of mapping wagon roads to California but with an eye to beaver pelts and Indian trade, such accounts as they did leave were not ideal handbooks for the prospective emigrants of '49.

Some such shortcomings apply to the other possible sources of information. The Santa Fe traders, even the few who had gone on to Los Angeles, had still missed the gold fields by five hundred miles, and could describe only a long, circuitous route. Accounts of the California marches during the Mexican War dealt likewise with a roundabout path to the gold fields and stressed military and political events. The best book on the Oregon Trail, Joel Palmer's Journal of Travels over the Rocky Mountains,[2] left the forty-niner to his own resources in the critical part of the trail beyond Fort Hall. Moreover, since it was based on Palmer's trip in 1845, it held out undue hope for profitable trade with the mountain men at the Green River rendezvous, and for supplies and fresh equipment at Fort Hall. A better guide was William Clayton's so called Mormon Guidebook,[3] which carefully traced the route from Council Bluffs to Great Salt Lake. But it also left off where the real difficulties began.

Frémont's reports circulated by the thousands and were the readiest source of information about the West.[4] Frémont, however, had traveled in circles rather than directly, making detours to climb mountain peaks and side-trips to examine the wonders of nature. His pub-

[2] Cincinnati, 1847.

[3] *The Latter-Day Saints' Emigrant Guide*, St. Louis, 1848.

[4] Especially John C. Frémont, *Report of the Exploring Expedition to the Rocky Mountains in the Year 1842, and to Oregon and North California in the Years 1843-'44*, Washington, 1845.

lished reports, furthermore, were based merely on his first two trips, in which he had not traversed the Humboldt Valley. They described, too, his crossing the Sierra in the dead of winter, when he had encountered difficulties probably far greater than those in store for the forty-niners, yet radically different. Consequently, his voluminous and brilliant reports, though a mine of valuable information for any western emigrants, were silent concerning the most crucial part of the most favored route, and were ill-arranged for those seeking compact advice. The sightseer more than the gold-seeker would appreciate Frémont.

Although most of the early California emigrants had not published any descriptions of the trail, there were a few. John Bidwell had prepared an abridgment of the journal he had kept as one of the leaders of the first group of pioneer settlers.[5] As far as Fort Hall along the Oregon Trail his pamphlet was fairly satisfactory, but he traced the rest of the route vaguely (his party having wandered uncertainly). And he was surprisingly casual about the Sierra crossing. Although his company struggled for three weeks to fight its way across, Bidwell wrote: "The mountains become low, so gradual, that you are at them before you are aware of it.—One day will take you to the plains of the St. Joaquin."[6] Lansford W. Hastings attempted to describe the direct route to California, but the description is not as good as for the trails he had traveled in person.[7] The nearest approach to a satisfactory description of the California

[5] Published probably at Liberty, Missouri, in 1842. See Wagner, *op. cit.*, pp. 49-51.

[6] Bidwell, *A Journey to California*, p. 30.

[7] *The Emigrants' Guide to Oregon and California*, Cincinnati, 1845.

trail was Edwin Bryant's What I Saw in California, *New York, 1848. Bryant did a good job of recording his experiences, and his breezy journal might have done excellent service as a guide-book had he traveled by wagon train instead of with pack animals and had he followed the regular route instead of the hazardous cut-off south of Salt Lake and across the Great Salt Desert.*

To summarize: Most of the accumulated knowledge about western trails was not readily accessible to those who planned the journey to California. According to one of the gold-seekers, "There were few, if any, who possessed a definite knowledge of the road and, as a consequence, there was great suffering."[8] *Although much had been printed, information about the overland route existed only piecemeal, and could not serve as a guide until ferreted out, sifted, and reorganized.*

Joseph E. Ware was the first to attempt a complete description of the best route for the forty-niners. His Emigrants' Guide to California, *published at St. Louis in the early part of 1849, was not only the first adequate guide-book but for several years continued to be the best in existence.*

Not having made the journey himself, Ware had recourse to the existing literature of the trails. Frémont's reports became his chief reliance, and to their use Ware calls attention as a vouchsafe of reliability. Sifting the essentials from Frémont's publications was a real service to the emigrant, and Ware performed it judiciously. Nevertheless, one must note that he did not achieve unvarying success, but lapsed into several errors. Since most of these mistakes, however, were in the minutes and seconds of longitude and latitude, users of the guide

[8] John Steele, *Across the Plains in 1850*, Chicago, 1930, p. xxxvi.

were not seriously imperiled. Although Ware mentions the use of "government data, maps, profiles, &c.," nothing in his handbook indicates that he had information concerning the details of Frémont's expedition in 1845, apparently nothing beyond the published reports of the first two expeditions.

Except for a general statement that he "sought, and obtained, information from various sources, private and public, that were known to be reliable," Frémont is the only writer Ware mentions. It appears, however, that he drew upon Hastings for instructions about outfitting wagon trains, used Bryant for the Humboldt Valley section of the trail, and copied, almost verbatim, Clayton's directions for the trail from Fort Laramie to Bear Valley, a stretch of five hundred miles, or almost one-fourth of the entire journey. From one standpoint, therefore, Ware's book is damned by his complete dependence upon other writers and by his failure to make adequate acknowledgment to some of his creditors in the lore of the West. It was not a great triumph in creative writing, even though a most useful synthesis of the best available information about the trail to California.

For guide-books, however, the criteria of evaluation are pragmatic rather than concerned with sources and literary etiquette. The forty-niners, looking for accuracy, completeness, conciseness, and grateful for any reliable travel information, were indifferent whether the facts were secured in the author's experience or by plagiarism, just so they were facts. On the basis of its utilitarian value the forty-niners judged Ware's Emigrants' Guide; we must evaluate it chiefly by that same standard.

On the whole it appears to have been trustworthy and helpful. Several suggestions, to be sure, may be questioned. *Some believed it a mistake to paint wagon covers. We may smile at the insistence on mid-morning baths. But concerning the major points experience corroborated Ware. The warning of probable congestion and delay at Panama was a cogent prediction. The overland route recommended was the most sensible, especially for the mid-westerners who were Ware's prospective readers. His was sage counsel about equipment, company organization, travel routine, health precautions; and the route was clearly indicated.*

Curiously enough—or perhaps naturally—the journals of the forty-niners seem to contain no explicit compliments for Ware's guide. With a single error more conspicuous than pages of correct guidance, the misleading statements were the ones commented on in the diaries. Two points in Ware's guide were the targets for practically all of the criticism. One concerned the length of the waterless stretch on Sublette's Cut-off. Ware made it thirty-five miles; one party found it fifty-four, others fifty-three, forty-four, and forty-one. Those who believed it farther, either because of taking a northern variant of the shortest route, or because the heavy sand on part of this road made it seem longer, suffered for lack of water and berated Ware in proportion to their sufferings. But since some parties reported the waterless stretch thirty-five miles long, Ware seems not entirely to blame. Again, Ware was criticized for his promise of good grass, good timber, good camps, and good roads along the Humboldt. Shortage of grass, brought on by the unprecedented number of cattle to graze in 1849, called forth such outbursts as the following:

"We all began to be greatly disappointed in our calculation of finding good grass on the Humboldt as Mr.

Ware had prepared us to expect. Let no traveller here-
after be governed by Ware's guide as it is perfectly
worthless."[9]

This wholesale condemnation, obviously exaggerated,
should really have been directed against Ware's lack of
foresight. He did not anticipate, either, the Humboldt
Valley's unusual wet season in 1850, which flooded the
lower roads and camps and placed additional difficulties
in the way of emigrants. Consequently, his portrayal of
customary conditions was the butt of caustic criticism
from the diarists of 1850.[10] *These criticisms rose from*
circumstances beyond Ware's control, though he should,
perhaps, have foreseen the possibility of a limited grass
supply becoming depleted. That he should foresee the
results of radical weather changes in an unknown coun-
try was expecting entirely too much.

In fact, it seems to me that the most valid criticism of
this guide-book hinges on Ware's failure to envision the
new problems that would arise with the migration of
1849. His advice was not attuned to the great movement
of the gold rush. In an earlier period the chief dangers
had been from Indian attacks or from losing one's way.
The gold-seekers on their way to California found the
Indians harmless, except for depredations on livestock
along the Humboldt; and as for getting lost, the only
ones to lose their way did so voluntarily.[11] *Delano gives*
this impressive picture of the great trek:

"For miles, to the extent of vision, an animated mass

[9] B. C. Clark, "Diary of a Journey from Missouri to California
in 1849," in *The Missouri Historical Review*, Vol. XXIII, p. 31.

[10] George Keller, *A Trip Across the Plains, and Life in California,*
Masillon, 1851, pp. 27-8.

[11] W. L. Manley recites two such experiences of his in *Death
Valley in '49*, San Jose, 1894, pp. 69-101, 109-278.

*of beings broke upon our view. Long trains of wagons
with their white covers were moving slowly along, a
multitude of horsemen were prancing on the road, companies of men were traveling on foot, and although the
scene was not a gorgeous one, yet the display of banners
from many wagons, and the multitude of armed men,
looked as if a mighty army was on its march."* [12]
In such a concourse the trail was unmistakable.

Two much more serious problems faced the forty-
niners—grass and disease. Both were products of the
crowded trail; the grass shortage obviously, and the
cholera just as surely. If the cholera was epidemic, as
most medical men believed, then the crowd was a medium
through which it spread rapidly. If it was due to contam-
inated drinking water, the throng was likewise responsi-
ble. Ware, to be sure, gave a good deal of advice about
finding grass and avoiding disease. Had he envisioned
fully the problems of the trail in '49, he might have placed
even greater emphasis here.

As the first guide-book covering in its entirety the
main overland trail, Ware's Emigrants' Guide to California has an important place in the literature of the
West. This priority alone would justify its reprinting
today as a document of the gold rush, even if the forty-
niners had in reality found it "perfectly worthless." But
as a matter of fact, it was not only the first, but one of
the few excellent descriptions of the trail. The emigrants
found no better complete guide until 1852, when Child
and Horn published their handbooks based on personal
experience, and until 1854 and 1859, when Steele's and

[12] Alonzo Delano, *Life on the Plains and Among the Diggings*,
Auburn and Buffalo, 1854, p. 46. See also Stansbury's description in
An Expedition to the Valley of the Great Salt Lake, Philadelphia,
1852, p. 24.

Marcy's appeared.[13] *For the first three seasons of the gold rush, and these three seasons represent the flood-tide, Ware's* Emigrants' Guide to California *was the most serviceable.*

The map and profile which accompany the guide are obviously based on the large map published with Frémont's report. The scale is the same, the choice of geographical features the same, and the entries on the profile identical even to the inclusion of St. Vrain's Fort, Great Salt Lake, and Carson's Lake, even though these were not on the trail described in the guide-book. To the map Ware added a rough sketch of the mid-western States, with routes to the frontier. He sketched in Sublette's Cut-off. In the Great Basin area, which Frémont had left blank, Ware entered the Humboldt River and the trail along it, but reduced the scale for this section of the map. Despite this inaccuracy Ware's map was an improvement on Frémont's, so far as the forty-niners were concerned, because it traced the complete trail to California. It enhanced the value of his guide-book.

Of Joseph E. Ware little is known except that as a forty-niner on the trail his guide-book describes he came to a most unfortunate end. I quote from Delano:
"But the most lamentable case was that of the abandonment by his companions, of Joseph E. Ware, formerly from Galena, but known in St. Louis as a writer, and if I recollect right, the publisher of a map

[13] Andrew Child, *Overland Route to California*, Milwaukee, 1852; Hosea B. Horn, *Horn's Overland Guide*, New York, 1852; John Steele, *The Traveler's Companion Through the Great Interior*, Galena, 1854; Randolph B. Marcy, *The Prairie Traveller*, New York, 1859. Wagner states that Horn's and Child's "are the first real guides, except Ware's," *op. cit.*, pp. 103-4.

THE
EMIGRANTS' GUIDE
TO
CALIFORNIA,

CONTAINING EVERY POINT OF INFORMATION FOR
THE EMIGRANT—INCLUDING ROUTES, DISTANCES,
WATER, GRASS, TIMBER, CROSSING OF RIVERS,
PASSES, ALTITUDES, WITH A LARGE MAP OF
ROUTES, AND PROFILE OF COUNTRY, &C.,—
WITH FULL DIRECTIONS FOR TESTING AND
ASSAYING GOLD AND OTHER ORES.

BY JOSEPH E. WARE.

PUBLISHED BY J. HALSALL,
No. 124 MAIN STREET,
ST. LOUIS, MO.

FACSIMILE OF ORIGINAL TITLE PAGE

We are authorised by
MAJOR S. P. SUBLETTE,
the celebrated Mountaineer, to say that the "Emigrants' Guide
to California" is accurate and complete in its descriptions,
routes, &c.

ST. LOUIS, MO.
PRINTED AT THE UNION OFFICE:
1849.

and guide-book to California. He was taken sick east of Fort Laramie, and his company, instead of affording him that protection which they were now more than ever bound to do, by the ties of common humanity, barbarously laid him by the roadside, without water, provisions, covering or medicines, to die! Suffering with thirst, he contrived to crawl off the road about a mile, to a pond, where he lay two days, exposed to a burning sun by day and cold winds by night, when Providence directed Fisher and his mess to the same pond, where they found him. With a humanity which did them honor, they took him to their tent and nursed him two days; but nature, over-powered by exposure as well as disease, gave way, and he sank under his sufferings. He told Fisher who he was, and related the story of his company's heartlessness. He was a young man of decided talents. Fisher was confident that if he had had medicines and proper attendance he might have recovered. What misery had not California brought on individuals?—and this is but one of many tales of suffering which might be told."[14]

JOHN CAUGHEY

[14] Delano, *op cit.*, pp. 162-3.

TO THE

HON. THOMAS H. BENTON,

SENATOR IN CONGRESS:

This little volume is most respectfully dedicated; from a conviction that the warm interest manifested by you on every occasion, in behalf of the inhabitants of the new territories of the southwest, will not be abated by a perusal of this feeble attempt to guide the feet of the hardy sons of the west, to the fertile vales, and golden hills, of our recently acquired possessions on the great Pacific.

Yours, respectfully,

THE AUTHOR.

INTRODUCTION

IN the following pages the author has aimed at one thing only—accuracy. We think we have succeeded in compiling a *guide,* possessing qualities more desirable to the emigrant, than any of the multitudes of books now flooding the country. We have had means within our reach, that could not be obtained by any of those preceding us, having the aid of government data, maps, profiles, &c., but a few days from the departments at Washington. Our distances are based upon actual survey, made by the talented Frémont. The altitudes, observations, &c., are from his pen also; to his mathematical precision are we indebted for the exceedingly accurate map of routes, profiles, &c. We acknowledge our obligations to Mr. S. Sublette,[1] for useful aid in the

[1] Solomon P. Sublette, a younger brother of William L. Sublette, one of the great figures in the Rocky Mountain fur trade. In 1849, Solomon married his brother's widow, possibly at William's behest, since he had willed her his considerable estate, four years earlier, on condition that she should not change her name. Chittenden, *The American Fur Trade of the Far West*, New York, 1902, p. 257. Though not so famous as his brother, Solomon had experience in the fur trade, and apparently in travel to California. Captain Sutter reported the arrival of the Sublette party: "Yesterday [October 7, 1845] Mr Sublette of St Louis arrived here with his party consisting of fifteen men. . . . Mr Sublette is a brother-in-law of Mr Grove Cook, and a man of considerable property. He intends to establish himself here when he likes the country. A good many of these emigrants have cash more or less, some of them several thousand dollars in gold. Not one company has arrived before in this country which looked so respectable as this." Quoted in H. H. Bancroft, *History*

enterprize, so generously offered. We have sought, and obtained, information from various sources, private and public, that were known to be reliable.[2] Hence, no part of the work is based upon conjecture. We make no claim to originality in any of the directions embodied in the routes, distances, &c. We are conscious some points are not as full as desirable,—their defects will be remedied next season, should the author feel justified from the patronage of the public, in having the entire route passed over by a Roadometer, with close and critical examinations of the various rivers, ascents, watering places, &c. —by a gentleman well qualified to accomplish the task. Such is our intention; feeling confident that we shall be remunerated in return.

J. E. WARE.

of California, 7 vols., San Francisco, 1884-1890, Vol. IV, p. 577. The next summer Bryant met Sublette and three others returning to Missouri. Bryant, *What I Saw in California,* New York, 1848, p. 110. Neither Bancroft nor Bryant records the given name of this Sublette, but with William and Milton dead I presume it was Solomon. The endorsement of such an experienced traveler lent prestige to the guide-book, but this seems to have been Sublette's chief contribution.

[2] Especially William Clayton, *The Latter-Day Saints' Emigrant Guide,* St. Louis, 1848; Bryant, *op. cit.*; Lansford W. Hastings, *The Emigrants' Guide to Oregon and California,* Cincinnati, 1845; and, of course, John C. Frémont, *Report of the Exploring Expedition to the Rocky Mountains in the Year 1842, and to Oregon and North California in the Years 1843-'44,* Washington, 1845.

CHAPTER I

TO THE EMIGRANT FOR CALIFORNIA

ROUTES

CORRECT information is of the greatest importance.—The distance is great, and in some respects, perilous. There are four routes by which the traveller may reach his place of destination. The first, cheapest and best, is across the plains and Rocky mountains; 2nd, by way of the Isthmus of Panama; 3d, by way of Cape Horn; 4th, through Mexico, by way of Vera Cruz. The expenses by all routes, except the overland route, will exceed $300. Our object is chiefly to furnish suitable information to the emigrant by the over-land route.

It is desirable that eastern emigrants who design making the over-land trip to California, should possess the most accurate information. Persons living in the New England States, as well as those living in the States of New York, New Jersey and Northern Pennsylvania, will find the route by way of the railroads, canals, &c., via Buffalo to Chicago, their best and quickest mode of getting there. We would advise such persons before starting, to dispose of their teams, wagons, &c., near their homes, as nearly every thing required for their outfit, can be obtained on as favorable terms in Chicago, as in any part of the east. On reaching Chicago, you can choose the route by the canal and Illinois river, to St. Louis, and from there up the Missouri river, by steamboats, to the frontier; or, by land, across the States of Illinois and Iowa, to Independence, or St. Joseph. The best place to cross the Mississippi is at Rock Island, or Davenport. The expenses on the route from New York to St. Louis, are nearly as follows: To Albany, fare one dollar; to Buffalo, by canal, five dollars: by railroad, nine dollars; from Buffalo to Chicago, steerage, six dollars: cabin twelve dollars; from Chicago to Peru, two dollars and fifty cents; from Peru to St. Louis, in cabin, five dollars: on deck, three dollars.

From St. Louis to Independence, or St. Joseph, distant 450 miles, in cabin, six dollars: on deck four dollars —the various prices along the route will be much reduced if opposition exists. If the navigation of the upper lakes has not commenced for the season, at the time you reach Buffalo, your course will then be to take the boat to Sandusky, and the Ohio river to St. Louis; or take the Detroit boats, and cross Michigan on the Central railroad to Michigan City; from there to Chicago, 40 miles, you take the mail steamer. The time required to travel from Buffalo to Independence, is about as follows: To Chicago by the lakes, 1200 miles, four days: by Central railroad, three days; to Peru, 100 miles, by canal, twenty-four hours; from Peru to St. Louis, 300 miles, two days; from St. Louis to Independence, 400 miles, three days and a half; to St. Joseph, 50 miles, 6 hours— total distance 2,051 miles—total time from Buffalo to St. Joseph, including lost time, eleven days. By referring to the Diagram of routes through the western States, subjoined, each individual can readily discover the shortest route to the frontier.

The rivers, when they can be used, are the most rapid and in some respects the cheapest route, as the roads at the time of your leaving home, will be almost impassable.

[2]

From Cincinnati to St. Louis, the charge for cabin passage is seven dollars: on deck, four dollars. Recollect again, you had better sell all your wagons and teams at home, unless you get a wagon made for the purpose; in that case, take it apart and carry it with you on the steamboat. If steamboats are generally adopted as the mode of conveyance, the Emigrant from the neighborhood of the Mississippi and Ohio rivers, and Lakes, need not leave home before the 10th of April; they can easily reach Kansas by the 20th of April. Those leaving the mouth of the Kansas by the 1st of May, in our opinion, will have the best time of it; the road will then be well settled.[3]

We will leave you to choose your own starting-point, simply stating that Westport, Independence and St. Joseph have facilities peculiar in themselves, for the outfitting of the Emigrant—every requisite for comfort or luxury on the road, can be obtained at either of those places, on nearly as low terms as at St. Louis.[4] You

[3] The emigrants had to wait until the grass was up, ordinarily about the first of May. In 1852, Child recommended that enough grain be carried to feed the teams for the first three hundred miles, making possible an earlier start. Andrew Child, *Overland Route to California,* Milwaukee, 1852, p. 9.

[4] These frontier towns, however, soon acquired an unsavory reputation. The following picture is of 1850: "St. Joseph is quite a village, and doing quite a great deal of business at this time; but the way they fleece the California emigrants is worth noticing. I should advise all going to California by the Overland Route to take everything along with them that they can, as every little thing costs three or four times as much here as at home. The markets are filled with broken-down horses jockeyed up for the occasion, and unbroken mules which they assure you are handy as sheep. It is the greatest place for gambling and all other rascality that I was ever in. We had to stand guard on our horses as much as if we were in the Indian Country. It is said that one or two men have been shot by the Emigrants, while in the act of stealing." Eleaser Ingalls, *Journal of*

[3]

would do well if you are crossing from the Mississippi, through Southern Iowa, or Northern Missouri, to get such articles as flour, bacon, &c.,—they will undoubtedly be cheaper on the road through to the Missouri, than when you reach the frontier,—as appearances at present would warrant us in asserting that more persons will congregate at these points during the coming, and succeeding springs, than the wisest foresight can make suitable provisions for. Your teams should be either oxen or mules. If oxen, they should not be over six years old, and not too large; the greatest difficulty may arise hereafter, unless you are careful at the start. Your time for starting from home should be arranged so as to be on the frontier by the 20th April. Your travelling parties should not be too large, not more than fifty men.[5] Do not be deterred by any stories told you on the frontier about danger, what others have done, you can do,—recollect one thing however, is certain, that you will meet with difficulties and trials. The question is not: how quickly can I get to California; there are other things to be regarded, the most serious enquiries are, as to the best, surest, and safest routes to be taken—what supplies you need to take along with you, and what provision you need to make for your future necessities. There is information to be had on all these points, and no sensible man will set off on so important an expedition, leaving anything to uncertainty or chance. From the best observations made we are satisfied that no person should attempt

a *Trip to California by the Overland Route across the Plains in 1850-51*. Quoted in Lorenzo Sawyer, *Way Sketches*, edited by Edward Eberstadt, New York, 1926, p. 17.

[5] Experience had proved larger numbers unnecessary for Indian protection and for cooperative tasks like wagon repairs, and in addition, they complicated the problems of water and grass supply.

to leave the frontier with more than lbs 2,500 weight, or with a team of less than four yoke of cattle, or six mules.[6] Let your waggons be strong, but light, with good lock chains, and the tire well riveted through the fellowes—if not thus fastened, you will have to wet your wheels every day, to prevent them from coming off. You want your waggon covers well coated with paint, and a few pounds to spare. You want good stout ropes, 60 feet long, with stakes about 30 inches long, having the heads shod with an iron band, with an *eye* for fastening your mules to, and probably your cattle. You cannot be too careful of your teams, to prevent their straying. Have also a spare chain or two,—if you intend to farm, you want the iron work of a plough, a set of harrow teeth, axes, hoes, cradle, scythes, &c., including a small cast iron *hand Corn Mill*—be sure to have a good draw knife and frow together with a few other carpenter's tools.[7] If you mean to "dig for gold," you want a short pickaxe, strong in the eye, a spade, several tin and copper pans, a meal seive (have a gold washing machine if you can afford it) of brass or copper wire; iron wire will rust—take spare wire webb along with you—see *yourself* that everything you want is procured; do not trust to others. Be sure to have a well bound cask 20 gallons in size, for supplying yourself with water, across dry plains. For

[6] Probably the commonest mistake of the forty-niners was to overload. The diaries are filled with accounts of heavy wagons sawed off or abandoned and of unnecessary baggage thrown away. Delano, for example, says that he "found the road lined with cast-off articles, piles of bacon, flour, wagons, groceries, clothing, and various other articles, which had been left, and the waste and destruction of property was enormous." Alonzo Delano, *Life on the Plains and Among the Diggings,* Auburn and Buffalo, 1854, p. 63.

[7] Gold was California's chief attraction in 1849, but its climate and agricultural resources were not entirely forgot; the forty-niners were not merely gold-seekers.

provisions *for each person*: you want a barrel of flour, or 180 lbs ship biscuit that is kiln dried, 150 to 180 lbs bacon, 25 lbs coffee, 40 lbs sugar, 25 lbs rice, 60 lbs beans or peas, a keg of clear cooked beef suet, as a substitute for butter (butter will become rancid in a few days on the plains), a keg of lard, 30 or 40 lbs of dried peaches, or apples, also some molasses and vinegar. For arms, you want a good rifle, and a pair of long pistols (some companies foolishly talk of taking small cannon along), or a revolver, 5 lbs of powder, "Laflin's" best, with 10 lbs of lead, and a few pounds of shot. If you have room to spare fill up with additional provisions, as they will be scarce after you get through; four persons are enough for one team. The first subject of importance in the mind of the enquirer, is, as to the cost of the outfit, &c. From careful estimate we arrive at the following result, and think it about correct. We base the calculation upon the supposition that four persons club together to travel with the same waggon. And below we subjoin a *second estimate* for three persons using oxen only, as a team— this is compiled by another individual, and for one year's provisions.[8]

[8] These estimates of the provisions necessary agree with the general consensus of opinion. Bryant, *op. cit.*, p. 144; Joel Palmer, *Journal of Travels over the Rocky Mountains*, Cincinnati, 1847, pp. 141-5. Apparently it was a mistake, however, to recommend the hauling of a year's supplies to California. Most companies discarded everything not essential on the trail.

For 4 persons, with Mule teams. Wagon, harness, and 6 good Mules.

Wagon,	-	-	-	-	-	$85,00

3 sett of harness, $8 each, $24; Mules, $75
   each, $450; wagon cover painted with two
   coats, $8. Total for team,   -   - $567,00

Flour for 4 persons,—824 lbs. at $2 per 100 lbs.						16,48
Bacon, do. do.	725	"	5	"	" "	36,25
Coffee, do. do.	75	"	7c	"	lb.	5,25
Sugar, do. do.	160	"	5c	"	"	8,00
Lard and suet, do. do.	200	"	6c	"	"	12,00
Beans, do. do.	200	"	40c	"	bu.	1,60
Peaches and apples,	135	"	80c	"	"	3,20
Salt, pepper, saleratus, &c. 25 lbs.						1,00

                                                $650,78

Cooking utensils, including tin plates, spoons,
   coffee pot, camp kettle, knives, and extras,   20,00

                                                $670,78

Making the cost to each one of the party,   167,69
From which deduct value of wagon, teams, &c.,
   at journeys end,   -   -   -   -   450,00
Leaving cost of travel,   -   -   -   220,78
Cost to each individual,-   -   -   -   55,19

ESTIMATE 2

For one year for 3 persons, with Ox teams:

Four yoke of oxen,		at $50,	$200,00
One wagon cover, &c.,			100,00
Three rifles,		at $20,	60,00
Three pair pistols,		at $15,	45,00
Five barrels flour,	1080	lbs,	20,00
Bacon,	600	"	30,00
Coffee,	100	"	8,00
Tea,	5	"	2,75
Sugar,	150	"	7,00
Rice,	75	"	3,75
Fruit, dried	50	"	3,00
Salt, pepper, &c.,	50	"	3,00
Saleratus,	10	"	1,00
Lead,	30	"	1,20
Powder,	25	"	5,50
Tools, &c.,	25	"	7,50
Mining tools,	36	"	12,00
Tent,	30	"	5,00
Bedding,	45	"	22,50
Cooking utensils,	30	"	4,00
Lard,	50	"	2,50
Private baggage,	150	"	
Matches,			1,00
One mule,			50,00
Candles and soap,	50	"	5,30
	2,583		$600,00

Cost to one man, $200,00.

Persons having families, with children, will find it necessary to make nearly as large an estimate for each child, as for an adult. Men, women and children, eat twice the quantity on the road that they would otherwise require at home.[9] Make no calculation upon any thing in the shape of game—you will need that too.[10] Do not encumber yourselves with any thing not absolutely essential to your comfort; take blankets, sheets, quilts, coverlets and pillows (omit beds), with oil cloth, or India rubber spread, to lay on the ground under you. Take no horses unless of the Indian breed; the common horse cannot stand the road. Do not start with the intention of changing your wagons, for mules and Indian horses at Fort Laramie, as recommended by one through the press[11]—it cannot be done—they are not to be had in any number. Cattle are best, except for packing over steeps. Oxen upon the whole, are the best; they need no shoeing, as the hot sand of the plain renders their hoofs so hard as to supersede the use of shoes. Some recommend cows, do not take them as a team.[12]

[9] From Hastings, *op. cit.*, p. 144.

[10] Earlier emigrant groups had subsisted largely by hunting. Few parties in 1849, however, killed twenty, ten, and twenty buffalo on successive days. Bidwell, *A Journey to California*, Liberty ?, 1842, pp. 7-8.

[11] In earlier years some emigrants had traded profitably at the forts of the fur traders and at the Green River rendezvous. Palmer, *op. cit.*, p. 145. In 1849, though, trade conditions were reversed; witness Delano's report about Fort Hall, "We had hoped to obtain some supplies here, but were disappointed. The company were even purchasing bacon and flour from the emigrants." Delano, *op. cit.*, pp. 141-2.

[12] One notes a general chorus of approval of oxen for the trip to the Pacific Coast. I quote from Peter H. Burnett, whose experience was on the Oregon Trail but whose testimony applies equally to the California emigration. "We fully tested the ox and mule teams, and we found the ox teams greatly superior. One ox will pull as much as two mules, and in mud, as much as four. They are more easily man-

Extra axle-trees are useful. Every mechanic should have his tools within his reach for emergencies on the road. Fish-hooks and lines are useful; seeds of most kinds are needed; all kinds of garden seeds, particularly peach, cherry, and plum stones—tobacco, cotton, rice, and other useful seeds.

For clothing, you want plenty of strong cheap goods, for hard service—as well as boots, hats, caps, &c. When rightly equipped, the undertaking is not so serious as may be supposed. One thing we would enjoin, particularly, *get up early* when on the route; start your cattle up to feed as early as 3 o'clock—start on your journey at 4—travel till the sun gets high—camp till the heat is over. Then start again and travel till dark—do most of your heavy cooking at the noon camp. *Never travel on the Sabbath;* we will guarantee that if you lay by on the Sabbath, and rest yourselves and teams, that you will get to California 20 days sooner than those who travel seven days in the week.[18]

aged, are not so subject to be lost or broken down on the way, cost less at the start, and are worth about four times as much here. The ox is a most noble animal, patient, thrifty, durable, gentle, and easily driven, and does not run off. Those who come to this country will be in love with their oxen by the time they reach here. The ox will plunge through mud, swim over streams, dive into thickets, and climb mountains to get at the grass, and he will eat almost anything. Willows they eat with great greediness on the way; and it is next to impossible to drown an ox." "Letters of Peter H. Burnett," in the Oregon Historical Society, *Quarterly*, Vol. III, p. 418. See also, Hastings, *op. cit.*, p. 145; George W. Read, *A Pioneer of 1850,* Boston, 1927, p. 60; Child, *op. cit.*, pp. v-vii; Randolph B. Marcy, *The Prairie Traveller*, New York, 1859, p. 28.

[18] A good many companies started out with the intention of laying by each Sabbath, "except when absolutely necessary to travel." But shortage of supplies, poor camping sites, competition for grass and water, and the feverish desire to get to California usually induced them to push on. Sawyer, *op. cit.*, pp. 25-6. Probably no company tested Ware's guarantee of saving twenty days by *never* travelling on the Sabbath.

CHAPTER II

DIRECTIONS FOR FORMING A CAMP.[14]

THESE directions are given on the supposition that you have organized properly, and that every member of the company is willing to submit to the orders of the Captain. Camps are usually enclosed by a "caral," or enclosure, formed by driving the wagons in an eliptical or circular form. It requires a little practice to make one at the commencement of the journey. By referring to the diagrams, Fig. 1, it will be seen that before you arrive at the spot selected for a camp, the wagon in the middle of the line strikes out to one side of the road, and is followed by all behind. By driving a little faster, the middle wagon soon gets abreast of the head of the line, thus forming two parallel lines; fifty yards from your camp ground, one of the wagons will be driven ahead and reined up square across the road, while the wagons following, divide their lines on either side, and take their places as indicated in Fig. 2. You will see from the second diagram, that in case of an attack by Indians, you can form a fort or barricade in five minutes, that no force of theirs could assault successfully. Cooking operations are generally carried on outside of the enclosures. Frequently you may have to drive your teams and loose stock into the caral, to save them from the Indians, who

---

[14] These directions, including the peculiar spelling of corral, are almost identical with the ones given by Hastings, *op. cit.*, pp. 147-9.

are ever on the lookout for plunder. From the moment you leave the frontier until you reach the Sacramento, you need untiring vigilance. The cattle are usually turned out soon to feed, whenever you stop to camp, where they are guarded by a company of "herds," detailed every day

DIAGRAM OF CAMP

FIG. I.

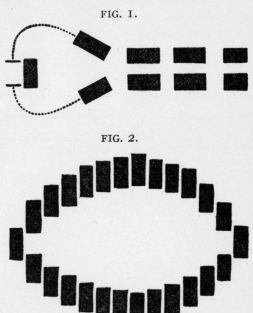

FIG. 2.

for the purpose. After feeding, if near night, they are driven into the enclosure, there to remain until turned out next morning by the herds, for the day. Designate your herds every night. It is necessary, frequently, to stake them inside of the caral. When it is unsafe to turn your stock out on the plains to feed, you will have to secure them with ropes, to stakes, driven firmly in the ground. The camp must at all times be guarded by sentinels, every man in the company taking his turn. No shooting of fire arms should be allowed, as false alarms are frequently raised by such carelessness.—Never allow guns to be capped or cocked in camp; deaths have occurred from carelessness in this particular.—Never allow an Indian to come within your lines under any pretext—they seldom have a good object in view.

They use every conceivable artifice at times, to elude the vigilance of the sentinels, often dressing themselves as various animals, so as to steal upon your cattle unawares.[15] When everything is ready for a start from the frontier, appoint a place as a point of rendezvous, for the persons to compose your party. Get out in the Indian country before you organise your company, which, proceed to do by selecting the best man in the company. Let him be cool, prudent and energetic. After travelling a few days, you have become acquainted with the qualities of the different men in your company. Elect the best one —let there be no electioneering for favorites—calculate to submit to the directions of the Captain-elect. If subordinate officers are needed, elect them.—As the best way, cultivate a spirit of civility and accommodation, let there be no contention or intrigues in your camp. If dissensions break out in your camp, separate peaceably.[16] Do not be in too great a hurry to get ahead. Everything

[15] Hastings tells of Indians masquerading as elk, *ibid.*, p. 149.
[16] The earlier Oregon and California emigrants had tested the organized company method and found it advisable. Although a few forty-niners "packed" through alone, the vast majority organized in semi-military companies. There was, however, no superior authority along the trail to enforce the company agreements and when dissensions arose, as they frequently did, the best solution was to dissolve the group. Break-ups and reorganizations were rather common. John Steele, *Across the Plains in 1850*, Chicago, 1930, pp. 57-9.

[13]

being arranged to your satisfaction, begin now to *"catch up,"* and move onward. From the State line to the Platte, a complete description of the road is not required. On one road the small streams are numerous, well timbered, and generally, in dry seasons, good to cross. Some few, where the banks are steep, will require some care. You will have to lower the wagons down into the creek on one side, and lift them out on the other. On the other route from St. Joseph, all the streams are bridged. You cannot, on an average, make more than fifteen miles a day. At the Kansas crossing, distance one hundred miles, you will find a ferry owned by two Indians. The charge for crossing is one dollar a wagon; horses, or loose stock, you can swim across. About ten miles above, there is a mission station of the M.E. church, where any blacksmith work can be done, which accidents may have rendered necessary.[17] The first stream of any size you reach after crossing the Kansas, is the Big Vermillion. Its banks are steep, the current is rapid, its bottoms are about a mile in width, covered in part with timber. Lat. 39.45.08.—W.L. 96° 32′ 35″.[18] If you have time you may get a meal of fresh fish here. Twenty-four miles further you cross the "Big Blue." Between those points, there is neither water nor wood. You must take enough wood and water to last you across. When you cross the Blue,

[17] At Big Soldier Creek. Bryant, *op. cit.,* p. 31. The forty-niners do not mention this mission, but report the Baptist Potawotami Mission, south of the Kansas and five miles west of present-day Topeka, and a Catholic mission station near present St. Marys. B. C. Clark, "Diary of a Journey from Missouri to California in 1849," in *The Missouri Historical Review*, Vol. XXIII, p. 9; Read, *op. cit.,* pp. 24-5; Kimball Webster, *The Gold Seekers of '49*, New Hampshire, 1917, p. 42.

[18] Frémont gives this position for his camp on the Big Blue twenty-four miles farther on. Frémont, *op. cit.,* p. 13. Ware used Frémont's figures carelessly, both in copying and in applying them.

you find a large spring of fine water near a creek. This stream is about one hundred and twenty feet wide, rapid current, gravel bed, timber plenty. If you find any of these streams high, you must camp and wait till they go down. If you conclude to cross at all hazards, cut down a couple of cotton trees, make "dug outs," place them eight feet apart, and lay "puncheons" across them for the wagons to cross on.[19] A good "pickle" can be made of the "prairie pea," which grows (on a vine similar to the common pea vine) in great plenty here, and is as large as a walnut. They are eaten in times of scarcity.[20]

COVE SPRING is about one mile up the stream. It is very beautiful. After passing several small branches of the Blue and Ottoe creeks, all having sandy beds, you reach the

LITTLE BLUE, twenty-eight miles from the Big Blue. It is fifty feet wide, timber plenty, grass and water good. You now are in the Pawnee country. Watchfulness is required to prevent their stealing your stock. Your camp must be well guarded every night, and your stock caraled, if necessary.[21] Your course lies up the

[19] Bryant's company, in 1846, crossed the Big Blue on such a craft. "We labored industriously the entire day in making 'dug-outs.' Two large cotton-wood trees were felled, about three and a half or four feet in diameter. From these canoes were hollowed out, twenty-five feet in length. The two canoes are to be united by a cross-frame. . . . This work being finished, the nondescript craft was christened the 'Blue River Rover,' and launched amid the cheers of the men. She floated down the stream like a cork. . . . Much difficulty, as had been anticipated, was experienced in working the boat, on account of the rapidity of the stream and the great weight of many of the wagons." Bryant, *op. cit.*, pp. 47-50.

[20] According to Bryant, Mrs. Grayson "made of the prairie pea a jar of pickles, and they were equal if not superior to any delicacy of the kind which I have ever tasted." *Ibid.*, p. 44.

[21] Frémont mounted his first guard at the Little Blue camp. Frémont, *op. cit.*, p. 15.

valley until you diverge into the high table land of the prairie. The valley is well timbered, grass and water plenty. Sixteen miles from where you leave the valley, you find both wood, water and grass tolerably good. The road is good. You find no water the remainder of the distance. Fill your casks.[22] The distance to the

PLATTE is twenty-one miles. Cook enough provisions for the distance. If the season is very dry, you better strike the Platte as soon as you can. You usually strike the Platte or Nebraska opposite Grand Island, twenty miles below its head. From the mouth of the Kansas to this point, the distance is reckoned at three hundred and twenty-eight miles. Lat. 40° 41′ 06″; Lon. 98° 45′ 49″.[23] Wood for fuel can be found on the island if the river is low. To the head of the Island, 20 miles, the road is good.[24] From the "head" to the forks of the Platte, 90 miles, the emigrant can supply himself with

[22] This advice was worth having, but some parties were unaware of the lack of water. "We then left that stream [the Little Blue], but not knowing that we had far to go without water, we did not fill our vessels. We drove 25 miles without water ourselves and but once for the mules." Read, *op. cit.,* p. 38.

[23] Distance and position from Frémont, *op. cit.,* p. 16.

[24] There is no mention of Fort Kearney, a military post established in 1848 on the south side of the Platte about ten miles below the head of Grand Island. The fort was an important landmark for the forty-niners, and because of its location near the trails from Missouri and Iowa it served as a convenient tallying station for the wagons moving westward. Captain Stansbury described it thus: "The post at present consists of a number of long low buildings, constructed principally of adobe, or sun-dried bricks, with nearly flat roofs; a large hospital-tent; two or three workshops, enclosed by canvas walls; storehouses constructed in the same manner; one or two long adobe stables, with roofs of brush; and tents for the accommodation of the officers and men. There are stationed here two companies of infantry and one of dragoons." Stansbury, *Exploration and Survey of the Valley of the Great Salt Lake of Utah,* Philadelphia, 1852, p. 30.

fuel from the island, or with buffalo chips [buffalo dung dried by years of exposure to the sun]. Buffaloes are sometimes plenty here. You have now been out more than a month, and experienced all the perils and hardships of life on the Plains. Many are no doubt down with sickness, mostly bilious complaints; many with rheumatism, contracted by being in the water much of the time.

To every one who designs crossing the mountains we would earnestly say, avoid large quantities of medicines, pills, calomel, &c.,—cleanliness and frequent bathing, are your best preventives of sickness—(never bathe if you feel fatigued—it matters not how warm you are, if you are not exhausted). The best time for bathing is about 9 or 10 in the morning; you are then stronger than at any other time in the day. Heed not the coldness of the water if it is soft. After leaving the water, instantly commence the most active rubbing, with a coarse towel, until a reaction takes place in the skin; dress rapidly, drink a good draught of pure water, and commence a smart walk until perspiration ensues; cool gradually, and our interest in California for it, but you will "throw medicine to the dogs."[25]

About a mile from the forks of the Platte, you will find a spring of cold pure water, drink carefully of it. On reaching the Fork, lat. 41° 04′ 47″—long. 100° 43′.[26]

[25] Compare with Bryant, *op. cit.*, p. 69, in which he cautions against too much medicine. "On this long and toilsome journey, during which it is impossible to suspend the march for any length of time, doses of exhausting medicines should never be administered to the patient. If they are, the consequences most frequently must result in death. The fatigues of the journey are as great as any ordinary constitution can bear; and the relaxing and debilitating effects of medicines injudiciously prescribed in large quantities, are often, I believe, fatal, when the patient would otherwise recover."

[26] Long. 100° 49′ 43″, Frémont, *op. cit.*, p. 21.

The trail lies up the south fork of the Platte, some distance to the crossing place. There is no fixed crossing place; it changes frequently during the season; cross where you can. There will not be much difficulty in crossing when the river is not high. When you enter the river, always incline down stream with the bars. The trail then crosses the prairie to the north fork. If there is no trail, cross the prairie anywhere. The distance across is 22 miles; if you cross above the bluffs, there is neither water nor timber, and the grass is thin. You descend to the valley through

ASH HOLLOW; by descending the bluff 5 miles above Ash Hollow, you avoid much heavy sand. The descent is good except in one place. There is a spring of good water here; the road for 150 miles now follows the Platte. From Ash Hollow the road is sandy; the wheels will sink in places from 6 to 10 inches; you will soon get over it. Springs are plenty, yet in many places you have to depend on the river for water.[27]

CASTLE BLUFFS are 7 miles from the Hollow. Timber is scarce for some distance onward; your main dependence for fuel will be on *"Bois de Vache,"* or Buffalo chips; wild sage is frequently used for fuel; it is plenty. Nothing of note occurs until you arrive at the

COURT HOUSE, OR CHURCH.[28] It is a rock, presenting an imposing and symmetrical architectural shape; distance from C. Bluffs, 53 miles; 12 miles further, will bring you to the

CHIMNEY ROCK.[29] An elevated mass of rock, hav-

---

[27] Based on Bryant, *op. cit.*, pp. 79-80.

[28] Courthouse Rock, about six miles south of the North Platte. So called because of a fancied resemblance to the court-house at St. Louis. Stansbury, *op. cit.*, p. 48.

[29] Chimney Rock, about a mile and a half south of the river. "The

ing a tall column-like projection near its centre resembling a chimney; it is about 250 feet high.

SCOTT'S BLUFFS,[30]—Are next in sight, distance 19 miles. The trail here leaves the river, and passes through the gap in the rear of the bluffs, over a plain for about 8 miles, you then begin to ascend toward the summit; when near the top, you find a beautiful spring of cold water; from the extreme right of the ridge, a fine view can be had of the Peaks of the Rocky Mountains. Laramie's Peak is about 150 miles west. Descending from the ridge, the road passes on to

HORSE CREEK over a sandy and barren country. —If the chance for camping is not good, you will find it a little better, 6 miles further, when the road passes near the river. From this point to Fort Laramie, there is no prominent object by which to remind the traveller of the distance he had travelled, excepting

FORT BERNARD,[31] 8 miles from Fort Laramie, it is a small, rudely constructed building of logs.

FORT LARAMIE and FORT JOHN[32] are about

rock much resembled the chimney of a glass-house furnace. A large cone-like base, perhaps an hundred and fifty feet in diameter, occupied two-thirds of its height, and from thence the chimney ran up, growing gradually smaller to the top. . . . It is a great curiosity." Delano, *op. cit.,* p. 71. Steele's descriptions are somewhat more concise. "It stands like a lone chimney sometimes seen after a building has been destroyed by fire." Steele, *Across the Plains in 1850,* pp. 66-7. "This . . . bears the unpoetical description of a haystack with a pole standing in the center of it." Steele, *The Traveler's Companion Through the Great Interior,* Galena, 1854, p. 17.

[30] Scottsbluff, named in remembrance of a fur trapper who had been left to die at this spot by his companions. Bryant, *op. cit.,* pp. 85-6.

[31] "A small building rudely constructed of logs." Bryant, *op. cit.,* p. 88.

[32] The forty-niners found only Fort Laramie, whose owners had purchased the other trading post and demolished it. Palmer, *op. cit.,*

one mile apart and west of the river. You now begin to cross the Black Hills, and will find some pretty rough roads, the ridges are high, and country barren. There is no difficulty in finding good camping places however; some travellers take the road that follows the river, and avoid the Black Hills,—it is said to be better travelling when the fords are good; the road crosses the river three times.[33] At a distance of seven miles from the Fort, you find a steep hill to descend; it is a long hill, and requires great care. Four miles and a half further, you find a steep hill to ascend and descend; the road is rough, rocky and crooked—half way over, there is a sudden turn in the road that is dangerous, if great care is not used. You leave the river at the fort, and do not touch it again for 80 miles. Two miles' travel brings you to the

WARM SPRINGS, and shortly after you come to

p. 28. Ware seems to be following Hastings, *op. cit.*, pp. 9, 134, 136. Fort Laramie's early history is beclouded by confusion in nomenclature. Originally Fort William, in honor of William L. Sublette, it was rechristened Fort John, after Captain John B. Sarpy, but eventually the clerks of the American Fur Company by persistently addressing it as Fort Laramie prevailed. Bancroft, *History of Nevada, Colorado, and Wyoming,* San Francisco, 1890, pp. 683-4; W. J. Ghent, *The Road to Oregon,* New York, 1929, pp. 133-4. "Fort Laramie is simply a trading post, standing about a mile above the ford, and is a square enclosure of adobe walls, one side of which forms the walls of the buildings. The entrance into the court is through a gate of sufficient strength to resist the Indians, but would be of little account if beseiged by a regular army. Its neat, white-washed walls presented a welcome sight to us, after being so long from anything like a civilized building, and the motly crowd of emigrants, with their array of wagons, cattle, horses, and mules, gave a pleasant appearance of life and animation." Delano, *op. cit.,* p. 76.

[33] Ware's description of the trail from Fort Laramie to Bear River, more than five hundred miles, is an abridgment without much change even in the wording of Clayton, *op. cit.,* pp. 12-18 and 23-4; plagiarism, but from the best handbook for this section of the trail.

a very steep bluff, the vicinity of this place is disagreeable on account of cobble stones in the road. By travelling 13 miles onward, passing timber and several creeks, you come to a creek on the south side of the road; it is a good place to camp. 13 miles further, brings you to

HEBER SPRING, near the timber on the right side of the road. There is a creek a few rods north from this spring. 2½ miles' travel brings you to a long steep bluff; you may have to double teams to get over this place. 15 miles ahead you find

LA BONTE RIVER, a fine camping place, grass, timber and water, plenty; the river is about 30 feet wide. A branch of the La Bonte, crosses 5 miles onward; the banks are steep. In the next 13 miles the chances for camping are poor; the road is but tolerably good. The curious may here look out for toads with horns. After crossing a few small creeks, you come to

A LA PRELE RIVER; it is narrow, but swift. The road from here to the upper platte ferry, 45 miles, is generally bad, being full of hills and vallies.

FOURCHE BOIS RIVER, 8 miles further, has steep banks, water good, some timber and plenty of grass.—You next reach the

PLATTE; timber can be found on the point, grass rather scarce, traveling heavy, distance 4 miles; grass and timber can be found on the point of the bend in the river.

DEER CREEK is 5 miles further, and a splendid place to camp, timber plenty, fish abundant, coal about ¼ mile up the east side; 7 miles from here is another good camping spot; after crossing a number of creeks, gulfs and ravines, you come to the

UPPER PLATTE FERRY.[34] Feed is plenty; timber on both sides of the river. If you conclude to ford, the best place is a little below the bend of the river. Seven miles ahead, the road turns South; road rather bad.— Five miles further brings you to a mineral lake and spring. Ten miles more will bring you to a piece of swampy ground, strongly charged with alkali. It is closed in with high bluffs; avoid it as a camping ground; do not allow your cattle to partake of the water.[35] To the north west, a short distance, you will find good water.

WILLOW SPRING is a noble spring of cool, pure water; it is a good camping place. Fifteen miles travel brings you to a creek on the left side of the road. The road runs parallel to this for half a mile.

At this stage of our directions we would take occasion to remark that it has been the practice of most emigrants to drive cows along with them, for their milk, (they are frequently their only dependence for drink, when crossing arid deserts on their route). The practice is a good one, but attendant with danger in particular stages of the route. After crossing the upper Platte Ford, the country, for over fifty miles, is volcanic in its character.—Water is sufficiently plenty, but it is so strongly impregnated with poisonous matter as to be dangerous for drinking purposes. Using this water, and eating the partially poisoned herbage of this district, together with the heated, feverish state, induced by

[34] Upper Platte Ferry, later to be known as Platte Bridge, and now Casper, Wyoming.

[35] Many unsuspecting emigrants realized this danger too late. One observation will illustrate. "Saw many skulls of oxen that died last season from the effect of this water. Saw one poor fellow standing at the roadside, one ox dead." Read, *op. cit.*, p. 66.

constant travel in the hot sun, renders the milk of such cows unfit for use. If you would avoid much sickness, camp fever, &c., abandon its use.[36]

We now resume our route. Eight miles from the creek you find a series of springs and lakes, highly alkalic in their nature. Grass is thin; no fuel but wild sage, (artimissia). Some supply themselves here with salarætus (carbonate of soda).

SWEET WATER is four miles further; current swift, with grass and water good; roads rather heavy. Your chief dependence for fuel for a great distance onward, will be on wild sage and willows. If you cannot ford this river opposite Independence Rock, go a mile higher up.

INDEPENDENCE ROCK[37] is well worthy the attention of the traveller.

DEVILS GATE,[38] five miles above the Rock, is a singular fissure through which the Sweet Water forces

[36] Bryant gives the same advice, endorsed by an army surgeon who accompanied Kearny's expedition to New Mexico and California, *op. cit.*, p. 108.

[37] Named by a party of trappers which reached it on the Fourth of July, about the normal time, considering its distance from the Missouri frontier. The names of William Sublette and Thomas Fitzpatrick are usually mentioned in connection with the episode. Bidwell, *op. cit.*, p. 7; Samuel Parker, *Journal of an Exploring Expedition beyond the Rocky Mountains,* Ithaca, 1838, p. 74; Charles L. Camp, ed., *James Clyman, American Frontiersman,* New York, 1928, p. 37. It became the rage to inscribe one's name on Independence Rock, so that De Smet called it "The Great Register of the Desert."

[38] The trail, of course, did not pass through Devil's Gate. "A crack or rent in the mountains . . . the surface of the walls showing that by some sort of force they had been separated, projectings on one side finding corresponding indentations on the other." G. L. Cole, *In the Early Days Along the Overland Trail,* Kansas City, 1905, p. 15. Delano observed that "it did seem as if his Satanic majesty had been cutting queer antics in this wild region." *Op. cit.*, p. 100.

its way. The walls are vertical, four hundred feet high, and composed of granite. The road runs near the river for ten miles from this point. In the distance of ten miles from this, the road crosses several creeks; grass abundant. After this, the road leaves the river, and is rough and heavy. Twelve miles from this place there is some timber. The road here again leaves the river for six miles, when it returns to the river again. You can avoid much bad road by leaving the old trail and fording the river. Sixteen miles travel from the timber, brings you across the river three times; the fourth ford is a good camping place. You now leave the river and do not find good water for sixteen miles. At this distance you cross the Sweet Water again; it is forty feet wide, two feet deep, grass and water, with willow for fuel. In the following five miles, you cross and recross the river to avoid bad road; near here the road crosses a branch of the river. Three miles from this brings you to a good spring—a little to the right of the trail. It is a fine place to camp.

SWEET WATER is fifteen miles further, and good for camping. There is much bad road in this distance; creeks are numerous, grass and water good. Ten miles further brings you to the

SOUTH PASS, distant from Fort Laramie three hundred miles, or about nine hundred and fifty miles from the mouth of the Kansas. Alt. 7490 feet; Lat. 42° 27′ 15″; Lon. 109° 27′ 32″. It is difficult, from the gradual ascent of the Pass, to find the precise summit; the point of culmination is between two low hills, about sixty feet high. The Pass is about nineteen miles in width, without any gorge-like appearance.[39] Between the Pass and the junction of the

[39] The description is from Frémont, *op. cit.,* p. 60. Unless Ware

CALIFORNIA & OREGON roads, nineteen miles distant, you will find the road good except in one ravine; water and grass good. To the

DRY SANDY, wood is scarce; wild sage will be your only fuel. Be sure to follow the road leading to the left, if you do not wish to follow the route described in the note. Sixteen miles further, you will find a good place to camp on the

[At this point we call the attention of the traveler to the note. The road to the right is an old trail. The present road is carried some seventy miles out of a direct course, by passing Fort Bridger. When you cross the Dry, or Little Sandy, instead of turning to the left and following the river, strike out across to the Big Sandy, twelve miles. If you get to the river along through the day, camp till near night. From the Big Sandy to Green river, a distance of thirty-five miles, there is not a drop of water. By starting from the Sandy at the cool of the day, you can get across easily by morning. Cattle can travel as far again by night as they can during the day, from the fact that the air is cool, and consequently they do not need water. Recollect, do not attempt to cross during the day. You strike the Green river a few miles above a small stream that comes in from the northwest. After resting a day at Green river, commence your route again. When you leave the river, keep a west, northwest course, to the branch; you strike it in about twelve miles by the trail; by keeping more west, you can reach it sooner. Follow it to its head, then strike across the high plain for the mountains, at the head of Thomas' Fork of the Bear river. Keep on the dividing ridge until you

allowed six minutes of longitude for the six miles between Frémont's camp and the pass, he miscopied the figures for the camp. Lat. 42° 27' 15''; long. 109° 21' 32''. *Ibid.*, pp. 60, 128.

come near the Bear river valley, then descend and cross down to the mouth of the Fork, when you find the main road. This is a fine road all the way; grass and fuel being plenty, and with the exception of the distance between the Sandy and Green rivers, there is fine water. By referring to the large map, you can see that you save nearly five days travel by following what I have taken the liberty to call *Sublette's Cut Off.*][40]

BIG SANDY. There is neither grass nor water in the next twenty miles, when you reach the

GREEN RIVER FORD—a bold stream, two hundred and fifty feet wide. If the Ford is too deep, go two miles higher up; grass, water and timber are good. For five miles the grass continues good; there is none then to be found for fifteen miles.

BLACK'S FORK is fifteen miles distant. Opportunities for camping are good, timber is not very plenty.

HAM'S FORK, four miles further, is a fine rapid stream, forty feet wide, grass good. Seventeen miles

[40] Sublette's Cut-off, sometimes called Greenwood's Cut-off. The estimates of the length of the waterless stretch vary amazingly. Delano, though he did not traverse this trail, makes it fifty-four miles, *op. cit.,* p. 120. Child gives the same figure, *op. cit.,* p. 31. Bryant says forty-five to fifty, *op. cit.,* p. 114; Horn, forty-nine, *op. cit.,* p. 30; Steele, fifty-three, *op. cit.,* p. 109; Clark, fifty-two, *op. cit.,* p. 25; Marcy, forty-four, *op. cit.,* p. 282; Sawyer, forty-three, *op. cit.,* p. 49; Read, forty-one, *op. cit.,* pp. 69-70; Palmer, who went over it twice, forty, *op. cit.,* pp. 34, 135; and Keller, thirty-five, *op. cit.,* pp. 20-1; likewise Leander V. Loomis, thirty-five, *A Journal of the Birmingham Emigrating Company,* Salt Lake City, 1928, p. 54. Apparently most of the emigrants found the distance greater than the thirty-five miles which Ware indicated, but they agreed that it had some good grass and excellent roads and was "not so much of a desert as a great deal of the country we have crossed." The Cut-off proved very popular; nine of every eleven teams in 1850 were estimated to have taken it. Read, *op. cit.,* p. 69.

further will lead you across Black's Fork three times more. The grass is good all the way; road somewhat heavy.

FORT BRIDGER[41] is thirteen miles onward;—you cross a number of small creeks. The Fort is a small trading post of four log houses; timber and water is good. Between the Fort and

MUDDY FORK, 13 miles, you ascend to the summit of a rocky ridge; route tedious. Several springs are found here, having a strong alkaline character. Twelve miles from the

MUDDY you reach the foot of the dividing ridge. Six miles further brings you through the summit pass to the

SULPHUR SPRINGS. The elevation of the summit is 8230 feet above the level of the sea, and is the highest land you have travelled over during the entire route. This is a connecting ridge between the Bear river or Eutah Mountains, and the Wind River chain of the Rocky Mountains, separating the waters of the Gulf of California on the East, and those on the West belonging more directly to the Pacific, from a vast interior basin, whose rivers are collected into numerous lakes, having no outlet to the ocean. The road is crooked and sometimes steep, passing between high mountains. Water is scarce during this distance. At the

SULPHUR SPRING you find good grass, and stone coal in the mountain side, a little distance from the road.

[41] "An Indian trading-post built in the usual form of pickets, with the lodging apartments and offices opening into a hollow square, protected from attack from without by a strong gate of timber. On the north, and continuous with the walls, is a strong high picket-fence, enclosing a large yard, into which the animals belonging to the establishment are driven for protection from both wild beasts and Indians." Stansbury, *op. cit.*, p. 74.

NAPTHA, or TAR SPRING is a mile off, in a South West direction; a wagon trail passes near it; it is well worth seeing; the tar is good for galls on horses or cattle. Two miles from here you cross the

BEAR RIVER.[42] The stream is here two hundred feet wide, and fringed with willow and occasional groups of hawthorns. This is a beautiful valley, three or four miles in breadth, perfectly level, and bounded by mountains one above another, rising suddenly from the plain. Alt. 6400 feet. From the entrance of the valley of the Bear river to

SMITH'S FORK, twenty-nine miles, the facilities for camping are good at almost any point. The valley, after passing the Fork, begins to narrow rapidly, and at the gap, is only five hundred yards wide. From here the road is winding, making many sharp and sudden bends. After crossing

THOMAS' FORK, ten miles distant, the bottom is unsurpassed in beauty. Wild flax grows here in great luxuriance; it is equal to oats for feeding to stock.— Rest in this valley a few days to recruit your teams and stock. Fourteen miles down the bottom, the road turns up a broad valley to the right, while the river passes through an open canon, where there are high vertical rocks to the waters edge. In crossing the ridge, the road is very steep for a mile. Distance around the canon, five miles. From the Fork to where you strike the river again, the distance is twenty-two miles;—timber and water are excellent here. From here to

BEER SPRINGS, a distance of thirty-six miles, the road continues down the valley, and presents an abun-

[42] Frémont's interest in the natural wonders of Bear Valley and his enthusiasm over its luxuriant grasses are reflected in Ware's description. Frémont, *op. cit.,* pp. 132-8.

dance of everything needful for camping. Beer Springs are so called on account of the acid taste and effervescing gas contained in these waters. They are a place of very great interest; some of them are thrown a few feet in the air, forming a beautiful *jet de eau.*

STEAMBOAT SPRING is supposed to resemble the puffing of a steamboat, and hence its name. Lat. 42° 39' 57"; Lon. 111° 46' 00"; Alt. 5.8. & 40.

Analysis of Beer Spring Water[43]

Carbonate of Lime, - - - - - -	92-55
Carbonate of Magnesia, - - - -	0-42
Silicia, Alumina, Water and Loss, - -	5-98

100-00

About four miles from here, the road turning to the right[44] leaves the Bear river valley for Fort Hall, and at a distance of twenty miles, crosses a ridge, which divides the waters of the great basin from those of the Pacific.

FORT HALL,[45] by way of the Port Neuf river, is

[43] Also Oxide of Iron, 1.05, *ibid.,* p. 136.

[44] A left-hand road, known variously as Hudspeth's, Myer's and Bear River Cut-off, bore off to the west, taking a somewhat more direct route to meet the Fort Hall road again at Raft River. This cut-off was popular in 1849 and the fifties. Steele, *The Traveler's Companion Through the Great Interior,* pp. 31-5.

[45] "Except that there is a greater quantity of wood used in its construction, Fort Hall very much resembles the other trading posts which have been already described to you, and would be another excellent post of relief for the emigration. It is in the low, rich bottom of a valley, apparently 20 miles long, formed by the confluence of Portneuf river with Lewis's fork of the Columbia, which it enters about nine miles below the fort." Frémont, *op. cit.,* p. 163. Today the site of the trading post is submerged under the waters backed up by the dam at American Falls. Ghent, *op. cit.,* p. 146.

[29]

about forty-five miles distant, or two and a half days journey for wagons. There is not much of note in this distance. The road in some places is heavy, and the chances for camping, generally, indifferent. Fort Hall is a trading post, situated at the confluence of Port Neuf and Lewis' Fork of the Columbia river, and should be occupied by Government troops, to afford protection and relief to passing emigrants. It is distant from West Port, on the frontier, thirteen hundred and twenty-three miles by the usual route. The ford of the Port Neuf is about one hundred yards. The

PANACK RIVER,[46] three miles lower down, is one hundred and twenty yards wide, bottom narrow and soft. After crossing the river, the road continues along the uplands; soil, clay. The immediate valley of the Snake river, (or Lewis' Fork) is a high Plain covered with black rocks and wild sage. The distance from Fort Hall to Raft river, is about sixty miles. This part of the route is particularly difficult—in many places the wagons will have to be forced up the ascent or ravines, by manual force;[47] grass is scarce. This part of the road is uninviting to the traveller, but yet, can be passed over without serious difficulty.

THE AMERICAN FALLS are well worthy of the travellers' attention.

FALL RIVER derives its name from the numerous falls;—many of them are old beaver dams, petrified. In

[46] Bannock River.

[47] "Some who have written 'Guides to California' describe the road from Ft. Hall to this river [Raft River] as being a very bad one, but if they were to travel it, they would hardly find the *desperate* places they describe. There is only one or two ravines in this distance and they are not at all troublesome." Keller, *op. cit.*, p. 25. But bad roads were reported here by Frémont, *op. cit.*, p. 166; and in 1849 Clark wrote, "Road very rough—country broken," *op. cit.*, p. 28.

its course from the Raft river, the road takes a south-western direction, and follows the trail across the dividing ridge to the head of Humboldt or Mary's river, distant one hundred and seventy miles. For two days you travel along the Raft river; camps good. The road over this distance resembles the country west of the South Pass in the Rocky Mountains for the same distance.— There are places in which great care is required, and some difficulty may be experienced in consequence of the unevenness of the road in passing over the dividing ridges of the mountains. On the

RATTLESNAKE RIVER you can find good camps; there are plenty of good springs also. The prevailing plant is the wild sage, which, in some places, will still continue to be your dependence for fuel, though there is some good timber.

We would earnestly advise you to oppose any experiments in your party, in leaving the regular route of travel to try roads said to be shorter. You will get to California in good season if you keep straight ahead. If not, you may lose a month or so of time, and experience the fate of the Donner's party. By trying a new road they lost nearly sixty days, and were overtaken by the snow, and spent the winter in the mountains, where nearly forty of them perished. Lose no time foolishly on the road, that can be spent with profit to yourself and teams.[48] You strike the

[48] Short-cuts repeatedly allured the emigrants, and usually the results were unfortunate. The Donner party, with its delay on the Hastings Cut-off, is the extreme example. Charles McGlashan, *History of the Donner Party*, Truckee, 1879; J. Quinn Thornton, *Oregon and California in 1848*, New York, 1849. In '49 and '50 the Hastings Cut-off enticed and disappointed others. Charles Kelly, *Salt Desert Trails*, Salt Lake City, 1930. Still other forty-niners experimented disastrously with variants on the Salt Lake-Los An-

HUMBOLDT RIVER at its head, from thence your course is down its valley for three hundred miles. It is the principal river of the great basin. It has been appropriately named after the *"Nestor of Scientific Travellers."* It has been named on the maps, variously, as "Mary's River," "Ogden's," &c. It rises in two streams, in mountains, west of the great salt lakes, which unite at a short distance below the trail around the south end of the lake via. "Mormon City of the Lakes." The mountains in which they rise are beautiful in their outline, and abound in wood, water, and grass. The surrounding country is a sterile waste, covered with a volcanic saline efflorescence. Its own valley is rich and beautifully clothed with blue grass, herds grass, clover, and other nutritious grasses. Its course is marked by a line of timber, mostly cotton wood and willow trees, and is unobstructed for three hundred miles, furnishing the requisite for the emigrants' comfort, in abundance.[49] From

geles route. W. L. Manly, *Death Valley in '49,* San Jose, 1894. The Lassen trail, another difficult byway, attracted many. Delano writes that although some of his company had misgivings, "the younger portion being fond of adventure, were loud in favor of the road," *op. cit.,* p. 179; but he goes on: "Instead of avoiding the desert, instead of the promised water, grass, and a better road, we were in fact upon a more dreary and wider waste, without either grass or water, and with a harder road before us. . . . We had been inveigled there by false reports and misrepresentation," *ibid.,* p. 181. On the other hand, some satisfactory improvements in the trail were achieved by similar experiments. Sublette's Cut-off, Hudspeth's Cut-off are examples.

[49] Some of the emigrants took violent objection to this description of the Humboldt Valley. "We had some grass here, but did not, as yet, see the line of cotton wood and willow trees, which is said to mark the course of the river. . . . From some cause we did not find much of the 'blue grass, herds grass, clover and other nutritious grasses' with which the valley is said to be 'beautifully clothed' . . . country a sterile waste, not 'furnishing the requisite for the emigrants' comfort in abundance.'" Keller, *op. cit.,* pp. 27-8. Ware may

the forks of the river to the "sink," the mountains are peopled by a race of Indians of the most thievish propensities, requiring, on the part of the emigrant, untiring vigilance, to prevent their stealing and killing their teams, &c. Their practice is to disable cattle, so as to make it necessary for the emigrant to leave them on the road.—Be always prepared to resist their attacks.[50] The road being level, and generally hard, enables you to travel over it with comparative ease. Occasionally, you have to cross the low sand hills, to avoid the canons, or to cut off bends in the river. Frequently, when the river passes through its canon, the rock approaches the rivers'

---

have exaggerated the "line of timber." Bryant wrote, "Clumps of small willows, an inch in diameter, with here and there a few wild currant-bushes, fringe the margin of the river, and constitute the only 'timber' that displays itself in this valley," *op. cit.*, p. 170. Yet Child promises "good feed all along the river, and excellent roads," *op. cit.*, p. 45; and Steele promises "plenty of grass and willows," *The Traveler's Companion Through the Great Interior*, pp. 39-47.

The forty-niners certainly found grass very scarce. "We all began to be greatly disappointed in our calculation of finding good grass on the Humboldt as Mr. Ware had prepared us to expect." Clark, *op. cit.*, p. 31. In 1850, the emigrants had to cut swamp grass along the northern edge of the Humboldt and carry it across to their cattle. Sawyer, *op. cit.*, pp. 79-86. Yet Marcy promised "Along the entire course of the Humboldt good grass is found in the bottoms . . . and good camps can be found at short intervals," *op. cit.*, p. 274. Many of the forty-niners would have preferred to endorse Horace Greeley's observation, "Here famine sits enthroned, and waves his sceptre over a dominion expressly made for him." Horace Greeley, *An Overland Journey from New York to San Francisco*, New York, 1860, p. 270.

[50] These were the worst Indians encountered. "This evening we passed a notice put up by a man whose name was Hendricks, warning Emigrants against the Depridations of the Indians, it stated that 10 horses, were stollen from one train, Eleven from another and all of another trains, also a man had been caught, and stripped of every thing he had on, Such is the character of the Indians with which we are associated at the present time it requires us to be on our Guard." Loomis, *op. cit.*, pp. 85-94.

edge, and may render it necessary to cross the river a great many times.[51] The soil is light and porous in many places,[52] making the travel bad on account of the continual clouds of dust arising. Many small hills occur near the road, covered with a basaltic debris. The entire country presents scorious indications. About one hundred miles below the ford numerous boiling springs occur, having a temperature sufficiently high for cooking purposes; they are indicated by the uncommon luxuriance of the grass near their edges. The emigrant frequently obtains mussels from the bed of the river; a soup of them answers very well for a change. Through all this valley you had better be on the road at a very early hour; the great heat of the sun, and continued clouds of dust, render it unendurable in the middle of the day.[53]—Rain seldom falls here. About twenty miles from the sink, or

[51] As a matter of fact there were two trails along the Humboldt Valley. Ware describes the usual trail, which was utilized throughout the forties, but in 1850 this road was under water and impassable. Ten years later Marcy described both routes. "The road, which follows the bottom, is hard and smooth, but can not be traveled in seasons of very high water, as the bottom overflows. It is then necessary to take the road on the bluffs, where the grass is scarce." Marcy, *op. cit.,* p. 274.

[52] "About the color of *good lye* from ashes," Keller, *op. cit.,* p. 28.

[53] A good forecast of the average experience of the forty-niners. "Our road today, though quite level, lay through a perfect desert, devoid of the usual dwarf sage, and covered with hot cinders and ashes. The sun's heat was intense; and the dust, mingled with saleratus, seemed intolerable. At times a hot wind swept across the plain, whirling the dust cloud mid-air, and as in playful mockery of our pain, pouring the hot ashes on our heads, until a person might have been excused if, in the delirium of torture, he had fancied himself in the neighborhood of the rich man's hell." Steele, *Across the Plains in 1850,* p. 186.

Some emigrants in 1850, however, had a very different experience. "About dark we were visited by a storm of rain for which we were well prepared, having already thrown away tents, wagon covers, and

HUMBOLDT LAKE, the road takes a south-west course, and crosses a barren plain having no water, and but few sage bushes for fuel; grass of an inferior quality—supply yourself with water. Some very large and remarkable petrifactions display themselves near the roadside on this plain.[54] After crossing the plain you reach the "Sink" (thus called from the river loosing itself in the sand at this place,) it is a low marsh, surrounded with bulrushes and saline incrustations and emits a most disagreeable effluvia; the water cannot be used for man or beast.[55] From this place to Salmon Trout river

extra clothing. We had supposed these things would be no longer required, as a 'guide' we had with us, contained the expression, 'it seldom rains here.'" Keller, *op. cit.*, p. 27. And farther on, after experiencing "cold rains nearly all day," this same diarist vented his sarcasm on Ware, "'The great heat of the sun, and continued clouds of dust did not trouble us *very much*,'" *ibid.*, p. 28.

[54] "Some remarkable petrifactions displayed themselves near the trail this morning. They had all the appearance of petrified fungi, and many of them were of large dimensions." Bryant, *op. cit.*, p. 188. The description of the "Sink" is also from Bryant, *op. cit.*, pp. 188-9.

[55] The "Sink" was the least pleasant part of the valley, but it was here that the emigrants said farewell to the Humboldt. Most of them did so in the spirit of the following lines, inscribed to Marys (Humboldt) River by one of the 1850 emigrants:

> "Meanest and muddiest, filthiest stream,
>   most cordially I hate you;
> Meaner and muddier still you seem
>   since the first day I met you.
> Your namesake better was no doubt,
>   a truth, the scriptures tell,
> Her seven devils were cast out,
>   but yours are in you still.
> What mean these graves so fresh and new
>   along your banks on either side?
> They've all been dug and filled by you,
>   thou guilty wretch, thou homicide.

the distance is forty miles, and must be performed in one stretch, as there is no grass nor good water on the road. About twenty miles from the opposite edge of the waste, you reach several warm springs; by cooling this water it is barely tolerable for drinking.[56] Then the road at times passes over high undulations, and all the distance is over a coat of dry ashy earth, so soft as to admit the feet of cattle ten or fifteen inches deep at times.[57]

SALMON TROUT RIVER [58] is reached near its mouth. This river takes its rise within 5 miles of the summit of the Sierra Nevada, and empties into

PYRAMID LAKE.[59] The name of this lake is de-

> Now fare thee well, we here shake hands
> and part (I hope) to meet no more,
> I'd rather die in happier lands
> than longer live upon your shore."

Horace Belknap, quoted in Loomis, *op. cit.*, p. 94.

From the "Sink" another road, used by many of the forty-niners, turned off to the left and reached California by Carson River and Placerville. The Truckee route described by Ware was somewhat better and more popular.

[56] "This is the most dreary desolate looking place we ever saw. It is on the top of a mountain and the water bubbles & boils up from the fissures in the rocks & forms into a small lake quite clear but so hot that it scalds." Clark, *op. cit.*, p. 39. Bryant reports, however, that when cooled this water "was more palatable to ourselves and our mules," *op. cit.*, pp. 191-2.

[57] From Bryant, *op. cit.*, pp. 189-94, Ware could have got a far more vivid description of this most critical part of the route to California. Marcy pays this desert stretch adequate respect: "The desert has always been the most difficult part of the journey to California, and more animals have probably been lost here than at any other place. The parts of wagons that are continually met with here shows this most incontestably." Marcy, *op. cit.*, p. 276.

[58] Truckee River.

[59] Discovered and named by Frémont, on January 13, 1844. He also bestowed the name Salmon Trout River. Frémont, *op. cit.*, pp. 217-19. Ware derives his description of the region from the same source.

rived from a bold pyramid formed rock standing in the Lake having an elevation of 600 feet, representing in outline and magnitude, the pyramid of Cheops, in a remarkable degree. From this point to the

PASS in the Mountains, the distance is only 80 miles.

SALMON TROUT, or TRUCKIE'S RIVER, (the name of this river is derived from the multitude of fish of that name that fill its waters, from Pyramid Lake to Truckie's Lake,) at the emigrant's usual crossing place is 60 feet wide, and 2 feet deep. It is 5 miles after you strike it before you come to timber. Its elevation at the mouth, is 4,890 feet above the level of the sea, being nearly 700 feet higher than the great Salt Lake, from which it lies nearly west, and distant about 8 degrees of longitude. Pyramid Lake is about 35 miles long, and rises about 12 feet above its present level, with the waters poured down in the spring, from the melting snows in the mountains. It is the nearest lake to the western rim, as the great Salt Lake is to the eastern rim, of the great Basin of the Rocky Mountains, and the Sierra Nevada.—The fish in the lake and river are of a superior quality, and extraordinary size, being generally from 2 to 4 feet in length, and form the chief subsistence of the people who claim the exclusive possession of the fishery. The Indians usually catch the fish by means of large traps, made of the twigs of the willow tree, growing on the banks of the river. If you have not lost time on the route, you would do well to camp for a few days to prepare your cattle for the ascent. From this place the road lies up the river; you will have to cross it between 20 and 30 times before you reach the summit of the first ascent, distance, 35 miles; this distance is over a good road, considering the elevation of the surrounding country, grass is very good, timber

sufficiently plenty for camping purposes.[60] On arriving
at the first level, you emerge into a noble valley,[61] walled
in on all sides by the surrounding mountains; the valley
is about ten miles across, and contains a variety of the
most nutritious grasses—timber is scarce, however. The
road runs across this valley, its centre is crossed by a belt
of slough or marsh; there will be little difficulty in getting through, the sod is tough.—On reaching the western edge, the road lies across a barren plain to the river;
on reaching the river, you will find it necessary to cross
it a number of times to avoid the walls of rock. After
following the river for some miles, the road turns off
short, through a gorge to the right, and begins to ascend
the mountain. The summit of the passage is reached at
a distance of about 7 miles; there is a good place to camp
on the top. You descend for some distance down a considerable steep, and find yourself in the second valley;
a beautiful stream of spring water crosses through its
centre. The mountains are well covered with pine timber, (*pinus colorado*) and the nut bearing pine, (*pinus
Monophyllus*) the nut is oily, of an agreeable flavor,
and nutritious, and constitutes the principle subsistence
of tribes among which you are now travelling. This
valley is also surrounded by high mountains; the road
then turns to the left. The country is very rolling, well
covered with timber, and occasional stretches of fine
grass. You find a small stream about 12 miles from the
2d valley, it is a tributary of the Salmon Trout. From
this to the head of

[60] Bryant, whose party traveled without wagons, called this trail
good, *op. cit.,* p. 198. But the forty-niners with wagons found it hard
going, with the road rough, and the fords "difficult on account of the
swiftness of the water and the number of large loose rock on the
bottom of the river." Clark, *op. cit.,* p. 42.
[61] Not far from Reno, Nevada.

TRUCKIE'S LAKE; the distance is about 25 miles, the country is composed of a succession of low hills, gradual in ascent in most places, grass good; you cross a number of small streams, and the main river a number of times, before you reach the Lake. This lake is the source of the river, and is about 5 miles long and 2 in width. This lake is called "Truckie's Lake" by some, after a half-bred Indian trapper, of that name.[62] Near the foot of this lake can yet be found the ashes of the houses built by the unfortunate Donner party, to protect themselves from the severity of the weather; they were burnt by order of Gen. Kearney, on his return from California in 1847. The road around the lake is bad on account of the swampy character of its banks in many places. From this place to the

PASS, the distance is but 5 miles. This distance is over a succession of ravines, and strips of swamp. You then reach the foot of the steep, over which you have to force your way.[63] We assure you that you will be tried to the utmost, in view of the apalling obstacles to be surmounted, but never despair, [if] others have [gone] over triumphantly, you can! Commence and unload, at once pack everything over the summit, on whatever mule you have in your party, then haul your wagons up the precipieces with ropes. By adopting this course you will certainly save time, and perhaps hundreds of dollars, from breakage of wagon, if not total loss of some

[62] Bryant gives a slightly different version, *op. cit.,* p. 202.
[63] Practically all of the diarists mention the difficulty of this ascent. "The road was very steep; in places passing over large granite boulders. Consequently we climbed slowly. . . . After resting awhile most of the oxen were attached to a single wagon, and with difficulty it was drawn up the precipitous ascent. This was repeated until all the wagons were on the mountain top." Steele, *Across the Plains in 1850,* pp. 212-13.

of your teams. Some have crossed, however, without unloading. Once on the summit, you can camp a while to rest. The elevation of the Pass is 9338 feet above the sea. This is 2000 feet higher than the South Pass in the Rocky Mountains, yet many peaks in your view are several thousands of feet higher still; thus, at the extremity of the continent, and near the coast, you witness the phenomenon of a range of mountains still higher than the great Rocky Mountains themselves. This extraordinary fact accounts for the great basin, and shows that there must be a system of small lakes and rivers, scattered over a flat country, and which the extended range of the Sierra Nevada, prevents from crossing to the Pacific Ocean. Lat. 38° 44', Long. 124° 29'. Thus the Pass in the mountain, so well rendered in English

SNOWY MOUNTAINS, is eleven degrees west, and four degrees south of the Pass.[64] You may now consider yourselves victorious over the mountains, having only the descent of one hundred miles before you. One mile from the Pass you come to

A SMALL LAKE. The waters here commence their descent towards the Sacramento from this place.— Your course is from the right of the Lake. A distance of four miles will lead you to a beautiful valley, having a stream passing through it. Grass of the most luxuriant growth abounds here. This stream is called

[64] The last four sentences are lifted *verbatim* from Frémont, except that Frémont gives the longitude as 120° 28'. After camping at the summit Frémont begins his next day's entry, "We now considered ourselves victorious over the mountain; having only the descent before us." *Op. cit.,* pp. 235-6. Frémont gives the impression that he ascended the Truckee to Donner Pass, which Ware is here attempting to describe, but in fact he crossed the Sierra farther south. See his map in *op. cit.,* facing p. 246; also Bancroft's *History of California,* Vol. IV, p. 438.

YUBA, from a tribe of Indians, inhabiting the valley lower down.[65] It is a tributary of the Feather River.— The road down the Yuba is very bad. You are now fast approaching the "gold region." Some think it will be found in plenty anywhere about your present locality.— You soon leave this valley and cross over the high strip of country to the

BEAR RIVER. Distance sixteen or eighteen miles. The bed and banks of the river are of a soft peaty nature. About five miles down the river, the road turns up the side of the mountain to avoid the canon of the river. This is a bad part of the road. After descending the mountain your course is down stream again for several miles. You then have to go round the river's canon several times, when you reach

LONG CANON. This you will have to avoid by ascending to the top of the rocky ridge. From this place the road recovers the river, and is pretty rough until you reach a part of the road where the ascent to the summit is difficult from the steepness of the mountain; on reaching the top if your wagons are very heavily loaded, empty them, and pack your plunder down, then lower your wagons down with ropes.[66] At the bottom load again, and in two miles you reach a beautiful valley having grass, and timber, in plenty. There are few points on the Bear River, where there is any thing like a valley, or bottom; it is a roaring torrent most of its course; its descent to this point is 3864 feet.[67] For 35 miles your road

[65] Bryant, in describing this valley, insists that Uber is the correct spelling, *op. cit.*, p. 206.

[66] Steele pictures just such a descent, *Across the Plains in 1850,* pp. 216-17.

[67] Frémont reports descending *to* an altitude of 3,864 feet, and his valley was on the American River, not on the Bear, *op. cit.*, p. 238.

[41]

is little better than what you have passed. When you come to a place where you can obtain a full view of the beautiful Valley of Sacramento. From this place to

JOHNSTON, the first settlement, is less than twenty miles. The road is good, and grass, water, timber, &c., abundant. Johnston's is located on the Bear River. You can be supplied at this place with fresh provisions, milk, &c., things of all others the most palatable. You need a day's rest here. From Johnston's to

SUTTER'S on the Americano, a distance of thirty-eight miles, you follow the valley of the Sacramento.— The road is good and needs no description.

SUTTER'S FORT,[68] is situated about two miles from the Sacramento, on a branch of the Americano. It was the property of the Russian establishment, called "Ross," and was purchased by Captain Sutter, together with its stock, agricultural, and other stores, with a number of pieces of artillery and other munitions of war. Sutter's Mill, where the discovery gold was first made, is twenty-five miles up the country, in the pine regions. From Sutter's to

SAN FRANCISCO, the distance is by land, *via.*

SAN JOSE, 200 miles. The Sacramento is navigable for one hundred miles above the Fort, for small steam-

[68] As Frémont had described it, "a quadrangular *adobe* structure, mounting 12 pieces of artillery (two of them brass), and capable of admitting a garrison of a thousand men," *op. cit.*, p. 246. The importance of John A. Sutter and his fort to the early American emigrants to California can hardly be overemphasized. Ware errs, of course, in identifying Fort Ross and Fort Sutter, the Russian establishment having been on Bodega Bay, almost one hundred miles distant. Yet it is easy to see how there might be misunderstanding of Frémont's statement, "the neighboring Russian establishment of Ross . . . sold to him a large number of stock, with agricultural and other stores, with a number of pieces of artillery and other munitions of war." *Idem.*

ers of one hundred tons burden, none of which have ever been used on this river. The year 1849 will form a new era, in respect to navigation in California; small steamers are building for the river, and the mail company's steamers will reach San Francisco, every week or two with the mails. It is most probable that any of the emigrants of this season designing to visit the bay, can, on their arrival, find daily opportunities on the Steamboats to do so, a route by all means the most desirable. At this point a great many will undoubtedly direct their course to the Gold mines, whilst others having agricultural objects in view, will seek themselves out a suitable piece of land on which to build their future happy home. May every just hope be satisfied. A description of the country is out of place here; the newspapers of the day have teemed with information on all the points in connection with this interesting portion of our happy Union.

Our object has been accomplished, we have given you a plain unvarnished naration of the trials, obstacles to be overcome by you in reaching the place selected for your future home. If we have erred in our description in any one point, we are sure it is a trivial one, and one of judgment, rather than intent.

A word before we part, you are now in a country different from that which you left. Recollect that you are a component part of the country. Take no steps that will not reflect honor, not only upon yourself but your country. Oppose all violations of order, and just law.— Unite with the well disposed to sustain the rights of individuals whenever incroached upon. Introduce at the earliest practical moment, those institutions which have conspired to raise our beloved country to the highest elevation of Nations:—Let schools, churches, beneficial societies, courts, &c., be established forthwith. Make provision for the forthcoming millions that shortly shall people your ample valleys, and golden hills—and above all, recollect that *"righteousness exalteth a nation."*[69]

[69] Compare with the exhortation to members of the Boston and California Mining Company by President Edward Everett of Harvard, to go to California "with the Bible in one hand and your New England civilization in the other and make your mark on the people and country." Quoted in O. T. Howe, *Argonauts of '49*, Boston, 1929, p. 50.

TESTS BY WHICH GOLD MAY BE DETECTED

EXTERNAL CHARACTERISTICS.—Gold is found native and alloyed with copper, iron and silver. Native gold is of a bright yellow colour, with a density of 19'3, is pre-eminently ductile and maleable. These qualities distinguish it from most of the other metals. Its primary form is the cube, but it occurs under several modifications, particularly the octohedron; it is also found in threads or stems, variously twisted, and in spangles, or rounded grains, which is proved to be its original form, instead of the effects of attrition. It is often combined with iron pyrites and with specular oxide of iron; also with tellurium and Palladium. The electrum, or argentiferous, is distinguished by its white colour, with an amber tinge, and contains in one hundred parts, 64 of gold and 36 of silver.

When gold is found associated with copper, or iron pyrites, the metal may not always be readily recognized, when fresh fractured; but on exposure to the air, the base metals become oxidized, whilst the gold remains unaffected, and becomes conspicuous, even when it constitutes only one-five millioneth part.

ITS GEOLOGICAL POSITION.—Gold is found in granite, as at Salsberg and La Gardette, in France, associated with beds of quartz and specular iron; in mica slate, as in Villa Rica, in Brazil and Virginia; in syenites and green stone, as in Hungary, Transylvania, and in Trachyte, a rock of comparatively recent origin, which is unknown in the United States proper. The latter rock contains the most powerful loads of gold, hitherto observed in place. In this rock are the workings of Kœnigsberg and Pelkabanya, in Hungary, and the best mines in South America. Our geological knowledge of California is not very exact, but we have reason to believe that it is from the trachyte the golden sands are derived. The gold usually occurs in veins of quartz, often resembling honey-comb, sulphate of barytes, or calcspar; it is, however, from the sands derived from these *rocks* that most of the gold is obtained.

CHEMICAL TESTS. BY THE BLOW-PIPE.—Gold and silver have a feeble affinity for oxygen, whilst the metals with which they are associated, such as copper, iron and lead, oxydise rapidly, and sink into a cupel of bone-ash; when exposed to strong heat, the gold and silver remains on the surface. A skilfull operator, therefore, with a Blow-pipe, a lamp, a piece of charcoal, with a little bone-ash bedded in it, will in a few minutes determine whether gold or silver occurs with any of the above oxydable metals. When copper exists with gold, about 16 parts are necessary to sweat out the former. One-half of this amount is all that is needed to effect the separation of silver.

BY ACIDS.—Gold is unaffected by nitric, muriatic or sulphuric, but is dissolved by a mixture of nitric and muriatic acids,—the *aqua regia* of the old alchemist. If the acids are strong, they have no effect whatever. Colorless aqua fortis, and ordinary muriatic mixed together, become yellow, and acquire the power of dissolving this metal as well as platina. Silver is readily soluble in nitric acid, and hence this acid is used to effect its separation

Bar Room in the Mines

Long Tom.

Lith & Published by Britton & Rey S.F.

From Huntington Library

Above, "Bar Room in the Mines," and below, "Long Tom."

from gold. This separation of platina from silver is effected by sulphuric acid, which dissolves the silver and leaves the platina pure.

By Mercury or Quicksilver.—Where the existence of gold is suspected in a strong Gangue, it should be roasted or burned, then pulverized and triturated with quicksilver, when it instantly seizes and amalgamates with the gold, however minute the particles. The gold is afterwards separated by distilling off the mercury.— Such are some of the ordinary and available tests by which the presence of gold may be detected. The explorer can procure a tin box and place the principal tests —lamp, blow-pipe, &c., in it, and strap it to his back; thus he will have a portable furnace, with which he can instantly accomplish an assay, or determine the nature of any minerals. Such an apparatus is worth all the books on geology and mineralogy that ever have been written.[70]

NEW METHOD FOR THE REDUCTION OF SILVER

Reduction of Silver Ores.—The following cheap and convenient test, in our opinion, is equally applicable for the purpose of reducing gold ore:

Two new modes of reducing silver ore, have been re-

[70] A dissertation on placer mining would have been of far greater use to the forty-niners. The first discovery and the first interest were in alluvial deposits. Although a tin box with "lamp, blow-pipe, &c., in it" might be "worth all the books on geology and mineralogy that ever have been written," the California prospector preferred "his washbowl on his knee." A year or two later one might have described not only the pan technique, but the cradle, the tom, the long-tom, the sluice, and other hydraulic processes. It was not until still later that quartz mining came into its own. Bancroft, *History of California,* Vol. VI, pp. 409-28; Owen C. Coy, *Gold Days,* Los Angeles, 1929, pp. 112-15.

cently introduced from Germany into Mexico, which promise ere long to supercide entirely the use of that expensive agent, quicksilver. The discoverer is a Mr. Ziervogle. According to the present mode the ore is first calcined with salt, which converts the sulphuret into a chloride; it [is] then at once removed from the furnace to a suitable tub, or other vessel, and a hot solution of salt poured over it which immediately takes up the chloride of silver and holds it in solution; the liquid is then drawn into another vessel, containing metallic copper, when the solution is decomposed, the silver being precipitated, and the liquid by a simple process is brought to its original starting point, and may be used over and over again with but little loss of salt. In the second process, ores or sulphurets are carefully roasted in a reverberatory furnace until they are converted into sulphates, when they are thrown into a suitable vessel, and boiling water poured over them, which immediately dissolves the sulphates; the liquid is then drawn off, and the silver precipitated by the same method as the first process. The latter process is best adapted for ores which contain a large portion of iron and copper pyrites as a certain quantity of sulphur must be present to ensure the conversion into a sulphate.[71]

THE ROUTE via CHAGRES AND THE ISTHMUS

This route is one that will be selected by a great number of persons, not accompanied by families, on account of the short time required for the trip. It has its advantages and disadvantages, and we will briefly discuss

[71] This advice, likewise, was not very appropriate to early mining in California.

them. The route would be from New Orleans to Chagres, thence across the Isthmus to Panama, and from thence to San Francisco. But little difficulty would be experienced in getting to Chagres, as vessels will be constantly leaving New Orleans for that port, but then comes the tug of war![72] Chagres is a mere collection of huts, inhabited by negroes, and numbers five hundred persons. A writer in the N. Y. Herald thus describes it: "Its climate is, without doubt, the most pestiferous for whites in the whole world. The coast of Africa, which enjoys a dreaded reputation in this way, is not so deadly in its climate as Chagres. The thermometer ranges from 78 degs. to 85 degs. all the year, and it rains every day.— Many a traveler, who has incautiously remained there for a few days and nights, has had cause to remember Chagres; and many a gallant crew who have entered its harbor in full health, have, ere many days, found their final resting-place on the dark and malarious bank of the river. Bilious, remittant, and congestive fever, in their most malignant forms, seem to hover over Chagres, ever ready to pounce down on the stranger. Even the acclimated resident of the tropics runs a great risk in staying any time in Chagres; but the stranger, fresh from the North and its invigorating breezes, runs a most fearful one."

Its accommodations for travelers, are said to be wretched; but from the above description, few, we should think, would care to task its hospitality. Should

[72] Ware's description of the Panama route is a rather uncharitable one. As a Missourian he probably was biased in favor of the overland route, and he may have wanted to discourage the use of any other. Some travellers by way of the Isthmus paint a less forbidding scene. Bayard Taylor, *Eldorado*, New York, 1850, pp. 9-30. Yet others found the delay and the climate at Panama fully as bad as Ware pictures it. Bancroft, *History of California,* Vol. VI, pp. 126-40.

a large number of passengers congregate at this spot and have to wait their turn in being conveyed across the Isthmus, as but one hundred can be carried daily, who can foretell the suffering that may, must take place. Companies would not leave their sick comrades or dying friends, and victim after victim would there find a grave!

The river journey is performed in canoes, propelled up the stream by means of poles. From Chagres to Cruces the distance is about forty-five or fifty miles. The traveler, who, for the first time in his life, embarks on a South American river like the Chagres, cannot fail to experience a singular depression of spirits at the dark and sombre aspect of the scene. In the first place, he finds himself in a small canoe, so small that he is forced to lay quietly in the very centre of the stern portion, in order to prevent it upsetting. The palm leaf thatch (or *toldo,* as it is termed on the river) over his portion of the boat, shuts out much of the view, while his baggage, piled carefully amidships, and covered with oiled cloths, *encerrados,* as they are termed, is under the charge of his active boatman, who, stripped to the buff, with long pole in hand, expertly propells the boat up stream, with many a cry and strange exclamation. The river itself is a dark, muddy, and rapid stream; in some parts quite narrow, and again, at other points, it is from three hundred to five hundred yards wide. Let no one fancy that it resembles the bright and cheerful rivers which are met with here at the North. No pleasant villages adorn its banks —no signs of civilization are seen on them; nothing but the sombre primeval forest, which grows with all the luxury of the tropics down to the very margin of its swampy banks; and the mangrove, and all the tribe of low bushes, which love to luxuriate in marshy ground, fringe the sides of the river, affording a most convenient place of resort for the alligators, with which the marshy country swarms. The sensible traveler, however, who remains quiet in his boat and makes no adventurous visits on shore, is perfectly safe from any harm from these animals, or the small panthers, monkeys, and deadly snakes with which the country on each bank of the river abounds. But those adventurous spirits who, here in New York, talk of landing on the banks and shooting game enough for their provisions, will find the thing to be impossible; as, even if they were to succeed in crossing the marshy banks on to firm ground without suffering from the alligators, they would find the forest so thick and tangled as to forbid further passage, and lucky indeed would they be if they got back to their boat unharmed by snakes or other poisonous reptiles. The journey to Cruces or Gorgona is not a long one. Of course its length depends on the heaviness of the boat, and the number of hands poling it up. A light canoe, with two active boatmen and but one passenger in it, will reach Cruces in ten or twelve hours, whilst a heavier one might require thirty-six hours to accomplish the passage. The passenger must take his provisions with him, as none are to be had on the river, and a good water filter will be found a great convenience, as the river water is so muddy that it is apt to derange the bowels, unless filtered in some way before drinking it. In view of the great and sudden influx of passengers to Chagres at the present time, it is impossible to say how they will all be accommodated with canoes, and what the river journey will cost. In former times the supply of canoes was quite limited, and the charge depended on the celerity with which the journey was performed. A doubloon ($16) was the lowest charge for a single passenger, and from that up to two, three, and four doubloons. As for taking out boats from here, and rowing them up the river, I should think it would be a hopeless attempt. Hardy boatmen from our south-western States, who are accustomed to a much similar mode of travel on their rivers, would probably be able to accomplish it; but in that burning and unhealthy climate, for young men fresh from the North, unacquainted with the dangers of such navigation, and all unacclimated, to attempt such a feat would be madness indeed.

Let us, however, suppose the journey completed, and our adventurers safely arrived at

CRUCES.

He may now congratulate himself on having achieved the most toilsome part of his journey, and but twenty-one miles of land route intervenes between him and the glorious Pacific Ocean. Cruces is a small village, situated on a plain, immediately on the banks of the river, which here are high and sandy. Gorgona, the other landing place, is a few miles below Cruces, and is likewise a small village, very similar to Cruces—in fact, all South American villages resemble one another very much. From these two points, both about the same distance from Panama, there are roads to that city, which roads unite about nine miles from it. Starting from either point, he commences his

JOURNEY ACROSS THE ISTHMUS.

The usual method of performing it, is on horse or on mule-back, with another mule to carry the baggage, and a muleteer who acts as a guide. The road is a mere bridle path, and as the rains on the Isthmus are very heavy, and there is more or less of them all the year round, the mud-holes and swampy places to be crossed are very numerous. Those who, here in New York, talk gaily of a walk across the Isthmus, as if the road were as plain and easy as some of our macadamized turnpikes, would alter their tone a little, could they see the road as it is. As for shooting game on the route, the same difficulties present themselves as on the river, viz: the wild beasts and reptiles with which the bush, or *monte,* as it is there termed, abounds, besides the great risk of losing oneself in the woods. Certainly, wild pheasants, guinea-hens, parrots, macaws, and a variety of splendid birds, unknown in these latitudes, do abound in the wilds there; but the difficulties in hunting them, are such as make it impossible for any save the native Indians to follow it with any success. The most rational, and, indeed, the only safe plan for the stranger to pursue, is to carry his provisions with him. That is the plan universally adopted by the natives, who would look on any one as insane, were he to propose to depend on chance game for his meals on the journey. Ham, biscuit, sausages, preserved meats, and such kinds of portable provisions, are the best to carry. As for walking from Cruces to Panama, in case mules are scarce, the feat is by no means impossible, provided the traveler arrives in Cruces in good health, and has but little baggage. It might easily be done with the assistance of a guide; but let no stranger, unacquainted with the language and new to such countries, attempt it without a guide. Having, then, fairly started from Cruces, either on horse or on foot, after a toilsome journey of some eight or ten hours, the savannah of Panama is at last reached, and the sight of the broad and glittering Pacific Ocean, and the white towers of the Cathedral of Panama, which are seen at the distance of about four miles from the city, give the now weary traveler assur-

[53]

ance that his journey will shortly end; and another hour's toil brings him to the suburbs of the famed City of Panama.

THE HEALTHINESS OF PANAMA, is far greater than that of Chagres. With due care, avoiding all excesses, and the night air, a person can preserve his health; still, the heavy rains and continual damp atmosphere, render it necessary to take every precaution; for, though healthy, when compared with Chagres, it is by no means a safe place for unacclimated strangers from the north.

And now, having taken the traveler for California across the Isthmus, let me conclude by giving a word of advice.

If he has a passage engaged through to San Francisco, the Isthmus route is decidedly the quickest, and, all things considered, the least weary.

But—and I speak now more particularly to those who have but a limited amount of funds—just sufficient to carry them through to San Francisco without any stoppage—let these travelers beware how they try the Isthmus, if they have only engaged passage as far as Chagres; after their toilsome journey to Panama, (if they escape delay and fever at Chagres,) they may have to wait weeks for a passage to San Francisco; and when the long wished for opportunity occurs, they will find themselves unable to take it, as their expenses in Panama, will have exhausted their means. Thus situated, in a strange, unhealthy country, moneyless and friendless, their spirits depressed by their situation, it requires no prophet to predict a heartrending termination to their golden schemes.

The distance from New Orleans to Chagres is 1,500 miles, from Chagres to Panama, 50; Panama to San

Francisco, on the area of a great circle, 3,450. The whole distance will occupy about thirty days.

The charges by steam will be as follows:

From New Orleans to Chagres, in Saloon,	$ 80	00.
Across the Isthmus,	20	00.
From Panama to San Francisco, in Saloon,	250	00.
" " in Cabin,	200	00.
" " Second Cabin,	100	00.

The following excellent advice from one who seems well acquainted with the route, we take from the New York Herald, of Dec. 23d.[73] It is clear and concise, and must prove of incalculable benefit to the emigrant:

PRACTICAL DIRECTIONS TO PERSONS ABOUT TO CROSS THE ISTHMUS OF PANAMA.—"1. Ascertain from the Consul of New Grenada, in this city, whether a passport be necessary. About three years ago the Grenadian government issued a circular to all its agents abroad, stating that such a document was indispensable to a foreigner wishing to land in the Republic.

"2. Upon your arrival at Chagres, take your baggage at once to the custom house, where you will experience but little delay. Then hurry out of the village, which is pestilential. Hire your canoe, which for expedition ought to be of small size. This is called a 'piragua,' is about 25 feet long, and navigated by a steersman and two rowers. The cost of boat-hire and men to Cruces ought not to exceed $12, unless, indeed, an increased traffic may have had the effect of raising the prices.

"3. Before leaving the vessel in which you arrive at Chagres, get the Stewart to provide you with a basket of provisions, sufficient for two or three days—such as cold

[73] Presented also in J. E. Sherwood, *The Pocket Guide to California,* New York, 1849, pp. 48-50.

fowls, or other poultry, hard boiled eggs, fresh meat, bread, a little tea, sugar, salt, &c. Milk may be procured at the huts on the river. Take with you an 'Etna,' or machine for boiling water, a tin cup, a knife and fork—in fact, bear in mind that you are to be wholly dependent upon your own resources.

"4. Avoid spiritous liquors and salted meats. A few glasses of good wine, to those who have been in the habit of using it, can do no harm.

"5. I would recommend every one to take from two to four grains of sulphate of quinine, the first thing in the morning, in a glass of wine, while on the river. Should you be detained in Panama, take a similar dose once or twice a week. This is the advice of the most eminent physicians in England.

"6. Do not sleep out of your boat, unless you happen to reach a settlement at night; bear the heat, bear the musquitoes, do anything rather than expose yourself to the night air, which is the source of every illness in that climate.

"7. There are two places on the river Chagres, from whence a road leads to Panama. Gorgona is the first at which you will arrive. Cruces is about five miles higher up. Your boatman will probably try to induce you to disembark at the former place; do not be persuaded to do so. It is further from Panama—the road is worse—the beasts are worse and dearer:—make them take you to Cruces.

"8. Take special care that your baggage be reduced into its smallest possible compass. A mule load consists of two trunks, one on each side of the animal, and you can put a bag or case between the two. The whole weight of the cargo not to exceed 230 lbs. Do not take large chests: they have to be placed crossways on the mule, cost double, and from the narrowness of the path, stand a fair chance of being knocked to pieces against the rocky sides.

"9. The riding mules will be hired to you with saddle and briddle, and the cargo beasts with their packs; so that you need not provide yourself with either. The proper price is $4.50 for the one, and $4 for the latter; resist giving more.

"10. There is but one hotel in Panama; the accommodation it affords is wretched and ruinously dear, the first charge being $4 a day: there are, however, many families who receive lodgers for $2 per diem, or even for less; these you will find out by inquiry of any respectable foreign resident, of whom there are several. Do not attempt to camp out, or live under tents; they have no idea of the climate who suggest such a proceeding. Even during the months of January, February and March, which are dry and comparatively pleasant, the attempt would amount to madness.

"11. The Patriotic doubloon is worth at least $19 in Panama; do not take less for it; the integral parts of the coin, of course, are valuable in the same proportion.

"12. Bear in mind these general rules. Avoid the sun; keep within the house during the day; eschew fruits, even when ripe; oranges in moderation may be excepted. Do not touch the oysters; they are very tempting, but from an intermixture of copper, are almost certain to produce cholic. Wear flannel next to the skin, by day and night. Be civil and courteous to the natives, and they will do anything for you."

TABLE OF DISTANCES FROM ST. LOUIS TO CALIFORNIA, BY WAY OF NEW MEXICO

To Independence, - - - -	400 miles.
Crossing of Big Arkansas, - - -	350
Bent's Fort (ascending Arkansas) - -	225
Santa Fe - - - - - -	270
Rio Del Norte at San Phillipi - -	30
Albuquerque crossing (Del Norte) - -	35
Descending right bank (Rio Del Norte)	210
Copper Mines - - - - -	75
River Gila - - - - - -	40
Pimo village (Indian habitations) - -	500
Mouth of Gila entering into Colorado -	165
Crossing Colorado - - - -	10
Crossing Cornado (first water) - -	100
First Ranchero in California - - -	65
San Diego on Pacific shore - - -	45
To San Louis Rey (Mission) - - -	46
Pueblo or City of Angels - - -	100
Santa Barbara - - - - -	100
Monterey (Capital of California) - -	310
River Rio Selina - - - - -	15
Rio San Joaquin - - - - -	85
Rio Tuwaleme - - - - -	12
Rio Stanishlow - - - - -	10
Sutter's Fort - - - - - -	90

Total distance from St. Louis to Sutter's Fort,
3,318 miles

This is a Caval [corral] that is best adapted to small companies driving large numbers of stock along. The reader will refer this to its proper connexion, on page 11.

FIG. 3.

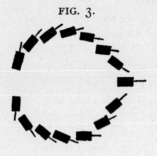

ALMANAC FOR 1849

MONTHS.	SUNDAY.	MONDAY.	TUESDAY.	WEDNESDAY.	THURSDAY.	FRIDAY.	SATURDAY.	MONTHS.	SUNDAY.	MONDAY.	TUESDAY.	WEDNESDAY.	THURSDAY.	FRIDAY.	SATURDAY.
JAN.		1	2	3	4	5	6	JULY	1	2	3	4	5	6	7
	7	8	9	10	11	12	13		8	9	10	11	12	13	14
	14	15	16	17	18	19	20		15	16	17	18	19	20	21
	21	22	23	24	25	26	27		22	23	24	25	26	27	28
	28	29	30	31					29	30	31				
FEB.					1	2	3	AUG.				1	2	3	4
	4	5	6	7	8	9	10		5	6	7	8	9	10	11
	11	12	13	14	15	16	17		12	13	14	15	16	17	18
	18	19	20	21	22	23	24		19	20	21	22	23	24	25
	25	26	27	28					26	27	28	29	30	31	
MAR.					1	2	3	SEP.							1
	4	5	6	7	8	9	10		2	3	4	5	6	7	8
	11	12	13	14	15	16	17		9	10	11	12	13	14	15
	18	19	20	21	22	23	24		16	17	18	19	20	21	22
	25	26	27	28	29	30	31		23 30	24	25	26	27	28	29
AP'L.	1	2	3	4	5	6	7	OCT.		1	2	3	4	5	6
	8	9	10	11	12	13	14		7	8	9	10	11	12	13
	15	16	17	18	19	20	21		14	15	16	17	18	19	20
	22	23	24	25	26	27	28		21	22	23	24	25	26	27
	29	30							28	29	30	31			
MAY.			1	2	3	4	5	NOV.					1	2	3
	6	7	8	9	10	11	12		4	5	6	7	8	9	10
	13	14	15	16	17	18	19		11	12	13	14	15	16	17
	20	21	22	23	24	25	26		18	19	20	21	22	23	24
	27	28	29	30	31				25	26	27	28	29	30	
JUNE						1	2	DEC.							1
	3	4	5	6	7	8	9		2	3	4	5	6	7	8
	10	11	12	13	14	15	16		9	10	11	12	13	14	15
	17	18	19	20	21	22	23		16	17	18	19	20	21	22
	24	25	26	27	28	29	30		23 30	24 31	25	26	27	28	29

INDEX

A La Prele River, 21
Albany, 2
Albuquerque Crossing, 58
almanac for 1849, 60
American Falls, 29n., 30
American Fur Company, 20n.
American River, 41n., 42
Ash Hollow, 17

Bancroft, H. H., xxi n., 20n.,
    40n., 47n., 49n.
Bannock River, 30
bathing, 17
Bear River, 20n., 25, 28, 41, 42
Bear River Cut-off, 29n.
Bear Valley, xii, 26, 28n., 29
Beer Springs, 28, 29
Belknap, Horace, 36n.
Benton, Thomas H., xix
Bent's Fort, 58
Bidwell, John, x, 9n., 23n.
Big Arkansas River, 58
Big Blue River, 14, 15n.
Big Soldier Creek, 14n.
Big Sandy River, 25, 26
Big Vermillion River, 14
Black Hills, 20
Black's Fork, 26
Blue River, *see* Big *and* Little
Bryant, Edwin, xi, xii, xxii n.,
    6n.
Buffalo, 1, 2
buffalo chips, 17
Burnett, Peter H., 9n.

California Road, 25
Camp, Charles L., 23n.

camp, directions for forming,
    11-13
Cape Horn, 1
Carson's Lake, xvi
Casper, 22n.
Castle Bluffs, 18
Chagres, 48, 49, 50, 54, 55
Chagres River, 50-1, 56
Chicago, 1, 2
Child, Andrew, xv, xvi n., 3n.,
    10n., 26n., 33n.
Chimney Rock, 18
Chittenden, xxi n.
cholera, xv
Cincinnati, 3
Clark, B. C., xiv n., 14n., 26n.,
    30n., 33n., 36n., 38n.
Clayton, William, ix, xii, xxii n.,
    20n.
Clyman, James, 23n.
Cole, G. L., 23n.
Columbia River, 29n., 30
Cook, Grove, xxi n.
Cooke, viii
cooking, 10, 11, 17
corral, 11, 59
Council Bluffs, ix
Courthouse Rock, 18
Cove Spring, 15
Coy, Owen C., 47n.
Cruces [Las], 50, 51, 52, 53

Davenport, 2
Deer Creek, 21
Delano, Alonzo, xv n., xvii n., 5n.,
    9n., 19n., 20n., 23n., 26n., 32n.
De Smet, 23n.